Opera Biographies

This is a volume in the
Arno Press collection

Opera
Biographies

Advisory Editor
ANDREW FARKAS

Associate Editor
W.R. MORAN

See last pages of this volume
for complete list of titles

SOME MEMORIES AND REFLECTIONS

EMMA EAMES

With a Discography by W. R. Moran

ARNO PRESS

A New York Times Company

New York / 1977

Editorial Supervision: ANDREA HICKS

————◆————

Reprint Edition 1977 by Arno Press Inc.

Discography Copyright © 1977 by W. R. Moran

Reprinted from a copy in
  The University of Illinois Library

OPERA BIOGRAPHIES
ISBN for complete set: 0-405-09666-6
See last pages of this volume for titles.

Manufactured in the United States of America

————◆————

Library of Congress Cataloging in Publication Data

Eames, Emma, 1865-1952.
  Some memories and reflections.

  (Opera biographies)
  Reprint of the 1927 ed. published by Appleton,
New York.
  1. Eames, Emma, 1865-1952. 2. Singers--
Biography. I. Title.
ML420.E17A3 1977   782.1'092'4 [B] 76-29934
ISBN 0-405-09676-3

SOME MEMORIES AND REFLECTIONS

"Nozze di Figaro"
Period Louis xv
1909

SOME MEMORIES
AND REFLECTIONS

By

EMMA EAMES

D. APPLETON AND COMPANY
NEW YORK : 1927 : LONDON

A PREFACE
Not an Introduction

On a night in August, 1890, I entered the Grand Opera House in Paris to hear Gounod's *Faust*, without knowing the names of the persons in the cast. As I was talking with my travelling companion before the overture began, a bearded gentleman in the seat directly in front of mine turned around and greeted me affectionately. It was Doctor Winfred R. Martin, now with God, but then the most learned man I had ever known. He was my teacher in Virgil in the Hartford Public High School, but had resigned this position in order to study Sanscrit at Tübingen. He was afterwards Professor of Oriental and Modern Languages at Trinity College, Hartford, and his extraordinary erudition was matched by an unerring taste in the fine arts. On this occasion he said, "You are in great luck to-night, for a young American girl, who has taken Paris by storm, is to sing Marguerite. Her name is Emma Eames, and she comes from Maine."

Indeed I was lucky. Emma Eames had not sung three bars before it was evident that she had the finest soprano voice I had ever heard. Furthermore, the part of Mephistopheles was taken on that memorable evening by Pol Plançon, who was later to delight two continents with his glorious singing and impressive act-

A PREFACE

ing. To see and hear, quite unheralded and unexpected, the finest prima donna of the 'nineties, together with one of the greatest bass singers of modern times, was certainly an unforgettable experience.

Emma Eames is my favourite prima donna, and I have heard all the best ones since the 'eighties. The last decade of the nineteenth century will, I think, be forever celebrated for its unparalleled constellation of operatic stars of the first magnitude. Lehmann, Ternina, Sembrich, Nordica, Fremstadt, Walker, Calvé, among the sopranos; and of men singers there were the incomparable Jean and Edouard De Reszke, Plançon, Lassalle, Maurel, and many others. Maurice Grau was quite right in advertising his operas with an "ideal cast," for if in the next world the angels sing as well as the leading men and women sang at the Metropolitan Opera House during the 'nineties, I shall be satisfied.

Now the reason that I place Emma Eames first in this magnificent group of sopranos is because she "had everything." She had a noble physique, ravishing beauty of face and expression, and a voice of apparently unlimited power and freshness. I liked her best as Marguerite and as Elsa, where the simplicity and austerity inherited from a long line of Puritan ancestors gave her a serene and statuesque splendour that I could not forget if I tried.

I am very glad that she has been persuaded to write her reminiscences; because she is not *vox et præterea nihil,* but a charming woman with a particularly well-furnished and interesting mind. On a solid founda-

A PREFACE

tion of Yankee ancestry and training, she placed a superstructure of French education and accomplishment. I do not know any one who is so perfectly at home both in Parisian society and in Maine villages. The story of her life would be compellingly instructive if she had never become famous; for she has a Continental brain and an American heart.

WILLIAM LYON PHELPS.

Yale University.

ILLUSTRATIONS

ix

Illustrations

SOME MEMORIES
AND REFLECTIONS

SOME MEMORIES AND REFLECTIONS

I

GREAT fixity of purpose, absolute absorption in the task in hand, and a complete obsession concerning the duty to be accomplished, have been the fundamental laws governing my career and life. Brought up as I was in the most Puritanical surroundings and nourished on Bible texts that were impressed upon me by my grandmother as being absolute working possibilities, my creed became: "Whatsoever thy hand findeth to do, do it with all thy might"—the unyielding command of that grim old preacher, Ecclesiastes.

Even when I was a child my grandmother's stern tutelage bore its fruit. When I was about ten, a small friend of mine came to visit her aunt in Portland, Maine, which was then my home, and it followed naturally that we often played together. One day, to keep us quiet, her cousin, a beautiful girl in the early twenties, gave us each a churn and some cream, explaining to us that by using the dasher diligently we could bring butter. My small friend, who, by the way, is now my sister-in-law and relates the story, soon became bored and abandoned her churn, but I stayed with mine, pounding that dasher up and down until my arms and legs and small back were one hot ache, and—the butter came.

In after life that fixity of purpose carried me through much that would otherwise have vanquished me.

I was born in Shanghai, China, on the thirteenth of August, 1865, the exact hour of my birth bringing me under the conjunction of Venus and Herschel, and dooming me, according to all the soothsayers, to great disturbances and violent happenings in all my personal life. Both parents were Americans, of Scotch and English descent with a strain of Huguenot. My mother was a great beauty, greatly gifted. She came of a musical family, all the members of which sang; which is undoubtedly why singing was as natural a function with me as any other.

In the early sixties my father, a graduate of the Harvard Law School, was practicing law in Boston when he received a most advantageous offer to go to Shanghai. He accepted, married my mother in 1862, and with her began the journey that was to take them across the Isthmus of Panama to the Pacific, where they embarked on the famous clipper ship, *Flying Cloud.*

In due time they arrived at their destination and were only too happy to set foot on the solid streets of Shanghai after their strenuous journey. And here it was that my brother, Hayden, was born on December 19, 1863; and about eighteen months later I came into the world in our home on the Bubbling Well Road that leads to the Rain God's temple.

We lived in a typical Chinese bungalow of the type that had been adapted to European needs. It was set well back from the road and approached by a winding driveway. There was a large bed of flowers just in front of the house, which contained many very sweet-scented Chinese and Japanese lilies. Their heavy perfume is still fragrant in my memory. The foundations of stone upon which the house was built contained openings shaped like keyholes which were most Chinese in character. I can see them yet, chiefly, I presume, because we children were most sternly forbidden to crawl through them and under the house where, no doubt, there were scorpions and other reptilian dangers, and my attention was thus emphatically called to their quaint contours.

A flight of steps led up to a veranda which encircled the entire house. A large hall divided this domicile into two parts. On the right were our nursery, bedroom and bathroom, the latter with great green porcelain tubs. These tubs my brother and I diverted to our own peculiar purposes, for our nurse used to make for us the most delicious rose cakes by placing the petals of the sweet-smelling Chinese Rosa Rugosa with a little sugar between sheets of clean paper and pressing them under these great baths.

Next to our bathroom were the dressing-room, bathroom and bedroom of my mother and father.

On the left of the great hall was a large drawing-room opening through wide doors into a dining room of formidable size. Then, beyond a tiny passage running at right angles to the hall, was the butler's pantry. From a corner of the veranda another flight of steps led to a low-ceilinged building containing an immense kitchen and the servants' quarters. At right angles to this building were the stables.

Then, turning one's back to the rear of the house one had, on the right, a rose garden and mound with an arbor covered with rose vines. Here it was that I first caught the delightful odor of willow twigs burning, a pungent fragrance that always brings back China to me. Behind the rose garden was a grove of beautiful old bamboos with a stream running through it, on which lotus grew. My nurse used to pick out the lotus seeds and give them to us to eat. They are supposed to assure one's return to the place where they are eaten —in my case, alas! an assurance not realized.

My Chinese nurse was a small or lily-foot woman of the better caste. She was more to me than the usual mother would have been or could have been who had any other responsibilities. She was sweet and gentle, kind and withal filled with the humor of life. My mother says she often heard her chuckling over me in the next room, saying, "Too muchee funnee chilo." The whole day long she would play with me and with my brother, who had outgrown the amah or nurse of his babyhood, and would watch over us at night.

The first sensation of fear that I can remember involved this nurse. I awakened suddenly one evening to see the grotesque shadow of her cap and shoulders upon the ceiling, thrown there by the light from an open fire, and I screamed with terror.

When I was a year and a half old I had pneumonia, so my mother tells me, and the French physician, the best to be had in Shanghai, pronounced me dead. The Chinese are well known to be perfectly devoted to children. Indeed, their love of children, love of beauty, love of grace, their respect for others and for themselves, and their absolute thralldom to their sense of honor made them, before they were corrupted by European commercialism, a beautiful and high-minded race. Of course, our servants were all Chinese, and when I had been given up for dead, my mother says, our Chinese butler rushed in, caught me up in his arms and took me away. When he brought me back I was alive. What he had done to resuscitate me my mother never knew and never could discover, but I have always considered it just another proof that that ancient race has known and forgotten more than we ever dreamed could exist, even if their knowledge does not include every wheel and electrical contrivance known to our civilization. And I have always felt that I owed my passionate love of beauty and grace to the fact that he may have breathed into me a small part of a Chinese soul to keep me sweet in an atmosphere in which I had to live later, of rigid, loveless, cruel Puritanism.

In those early days there were no cows in China. Instead, gray buffaloes were brought into the courtyard and milked for us. The Bubbling Well Road on which we lived then ran just outside the city, but to-day it is included in Shanghai proper. My father drove in and out to his office, while my mother rode in a sedan chair along streets where now I imagine a stream of motors rushes, as in all other countries. Such a peaceful, quiet life, in which there were no unpleasant things to remember except two moments of childish panic!

The first of these was, of course, my fright at the shadow of my nurse, a grotesquerie thrown by the firelight on to the ceiling; and the second came as a sort of natural consequence of disobedience. My nurse had left me for a moment, and resenting this desertion I started after her to the servants' quarters. I got as far as the veranda when I saw two great green eyes looking at me out of the black night—some dog strayed away, probably, but to my childish mind a monstrous beast come to devour me. I shrieked and fled back to the nursery and safety.

Of my mother, I remember little as a child, for she was tremendously absorbed by her social duties. She was much in demand socially, being very beautiful with an exquisitely pale, lily-like complexion, great blue eyes—perfect in feature and figure and with an infinite charm of manner. Beautifully dressed, too, because what her sewing man—there were no women dressmakers in China—could not make for her, she had sent out from Paris. Added to her social duties she had a musical one, that of playing the piano and singing with an amateur orchestra.

She had many friends, and once one of them gave me a mechanical toy from Paris consisting of a beautiful lady, finely dressed, seated in a victoria with coachman, horse and all complete. As her equipage advanced, this beautiful lady bowed first to the right and then to the left as long as the victoria was in motion.

How I hated that toy! How that eternal bowing bored me! For the pretty lady with her unceasing genuflexions gave me no opportunity to imagine her doing anything else, appearing in any other rôle, and I despised her

8

accordingly. That toy, I firmly believe, witnessed the birth of my horror of the mechanical.

The toy I adored, a doll called Violet, had no such limitations. Violet had blond hair, real hair that I could dress in any way that I wished, and beautiful blue eyes, a porcelain head and a kid body. There was nothing that could not be imagined about this charming person. I even dressed her as a baby if I wished. I always felt—and feel to this day—that there was something alive in that little kid body that I cherished.

Later, one of the first cataclysms of my existence was brought about by Violet. An unimaginative and rather hard friend of my mother, seeing that Violet's kid finger had gone the way of doll's flesh, and that one eye had sunk into her head, threw the doll away. It was my first great bereavement, although I was then nine and ready to do without dolls. But she was my first doll, and the only pet I ever had that did not have four legs. And whenever afterwards I sang Nevin's "I once had a sweet little doll, dears," I always thought of Violet and was on the verge of tears.

The only snow we had in Shanghai was a

few flakes that melted as soon as they fell; and the only Christmas celebrations we knew were the entertainments of the Chinese jugglers who performed at our Christmas parties.

Of my father only the vaguest memory remains. He was, of course, busy in town all day and came home only after his children had been put to bed. I do recall that he often said: "Funny child, she must be double-jointed!" a remark called forth, I suppose, by my doing a complete "split" on any and every occasion without having had any instruction in that gymnastic feat.

The meaning of a lie was first taught me in China when I was a baby. Just what the particular lie was that brought about my enlightenment I do not remember, but my mother took me into her room with a very serious face and told me that I had soiled my mouth by telling an untruth. Then with a towel and some ashes from the grate, she scoured out my mouth to impress upon me the uncleanness of my sin.

My first lesson in fortitude was attended by circumstances almost as painful. I had fallen down and hurt myself quite badly. Scrambling to my feet, I began to howl vigorously. My father, attracted by the uproar, admonished me, saying: "Brave little girls don't cry when they are hurt!" I remember I stopped instantly, struck by the word brave. And it immediately sank into my consciousness, never to leave it, that "brave" was the desirable, the necessary thing to be.

It was always like that with me. Every impression of any kind always aroused an intense reaction. I realized in later years that this was one way in which I was wasting myself, and that I must put a stop to it as a matter of emotional self-preservation. A great river overflowing its banks must be canalized to make it safe and usable. It is the same with one's emotions if one wants to use them instead of being ruled by them—or if, as Hugh Walpole puts it, one prefers to "ride one's tiger."

It has been said that the year Barnum brought Tom Thumb to China was 1872, but I remember attending a matinée with all the other children of the foreign colony in Shanghai given by this famous troupe, including Tom Thumb, Minnie Warren, and Commodore Nutt, in 1870. It was at this performance that I was placed on the stage as one of the children to whom these midgets might be compared in size and general build; and the first thing I did after being set down was to make a wild dash for the scandalized dwarfs and, clutching them in my arms, beg them to come home with me and be my dollies.

They were perfectly outraged at the insult, naturally, and I was separated from them forcibly and, be it said, only with the greatest difficulty, shrieking and almost heartbroken at being torn from them. I can yet feel the tremendous emotion I experienced at seeing them, and believing that at last some dollies had come to life to play with me; an emotion that blinded me to their very obvious hideousness.

In the present age—a blend of realism and positivism—much that is false has been swept away, and much that is foul and unclean has been brought to the surface in the upheaval. Out of this have come different values of life and living, of our duty to our neighbor and his to us; but, nevertheless, I am glad that I was of my period; that I believed fervently and passionately in fairies, in Santa Claus, and all the myths that bring poetry and beauty into the lives of imaginative children. Such crimes committed by minors as are filling the police calendar to-day would have been impossible to the children who were my contemporaries.

MRS. EAMES
1892

EMMA EAMES AT THE AGE OF
SIX YEARS

Some Memories and Reflections

When I was about four years old we paid a visit to some friends of my mother in Yokohama—charming English people named Hepburn. One morning while with them I heard strains of music—the music of a regimental band, I was told afterwards—so heart-breaking that I rushed to the window and stood sobbing as I watched the procession passing. I have a distinct vision yet of the officer's charger being led at this funeral; and the choking agony of emotion that came over me at this, my first hearing of Chopin's Funeral March is still a vivid memory. And no matter where I hear it played to-day the vision of that charger, carrying his master's sword and his boots reversed, pacing slowly under that Yokohama window, comes before me.

It was during those early years that, so Mamma tells me, my brother and I used to burst into tears when she sang, and say, "Oh, Mamma, Mamma, don't, don't! You have such a lonesome voice," because we were so touched by its sympathetic quality.

As for myself, I always sang as a child, sang when I was happy, when I was playing or just daydreaming—wandering little tunes that somehow had found their way into my throat, or else a busy, contented little humming. I never thought of it as singing, however; never was conscious of my voice. When I was a child in Bath, Maine, I had a playmate—I can hardly call her a friend—who had an exquisite, flute-like soprano voice; and my grandmother always said that she wished I had a nice, ladylike voice like Jennie's instead of a great loud one like mine!

Of those first five years of my life which were spent in China my most vivid remembrances are, strangely enough, sensations and emotions rather than the facts that caused them.

I do recall one concrete act, however, a naughtiness that I committed. As my memory brings everything back to me in pictures, I can see myself yet sitting in a big chair, screaming at my Chinese nurse as she tried to put some pretty openwork silk socks on my kicking feet. I howled that I would not wear them—no, I would not! And being at the inarticulate age I could not explain that it was because the openwork part hurt my feet.

It is a catastrophe to be so sensitive. I was always so, in mind and heart as well as body. Mentally and spiritually I have always been like a person who walked through a crowd on tender feet and dreaded their being bruised; a fact that explains, perhaps, why so many called me cold, aloof, proud. My dread of being hurt had thrown up a wall of great reserve about me without my being conscious of it.

In 1870 we were compelled to leave China on account of my mother's health. She was not at all well, and felt that she could obtain proper medical treatment only in France. All plans had been made by my mother to take us to Mentone for our education. The outbreak of the Franco-Prussian War necessitated a complete change of plan and we returned to Bath, Maine, to the house of my mother's parents until Mamma could arrange for a home in Portland, Maine, where we lived for four years. Although I never returned, it seems that China never quite forgot me. For years after I had left Shanghai, at the height of my career, I was most touched to have Mrs. Hitt the elder, wife of the senator, tell me of meeting a distinguished Chinese diplomat on the steamer returning from Hawaii and having him remark in the course of a conversation on art and letters: "You know your Emma Eames is a compatriot of ours."

Only one incident of the voyage from China lingers with me. A kindly Frenchman, seeing us very much bored at the monotony of the trip and at loose ends for something to do, took my brother and me into his cabin—how well I remember that dark little room with its flickering lamp!—and emptied the contents of his toilet case for our amusement. And among the lotions and creams and soaps and toilet waters, I became entranced with a stick of pomade because of its delicious perfume, which I afterward discovered was heliotrope.

When we arrived in San Francisco we stopped at the Palace Hotel. And, having just come from Shanghai, one of the servants thought it amusing to call my brother a Shanghai rooster. Whereupon, perfectly infuriated at the insult, I leaped upon the poor man and attempted to demolish him. It is the first rage that I can remember. Incidentally, it is an interesting insight into child psychology to note that in China, where I was surrounded by love and sweetness and understanding, I was the most docile and loving of children, but when I returned to America and encountered that peculiar kind of teasing, particularly of my brother, it aroused a perfect devil in me.

During the remaining period, until I was eleven, there is little that is interesting to recount. There were, of course, rough games with my brother—who was about a year and a half older than I and who always had an eye to my care—and his friends. But my favorite game was "playing theater," as I called it. This consisted of working out plots and improvising emotional situations as I went along, and taking the latter so much to heart that I would arrive at such a point of feverish excitement and wild sobs that I had to be put to bed to cool off.

One of the greatest joys I had during those years was being taken to see a melodrama called "The Sea of Ice." I have always loved acting and the theater; and had I been an actress and not an opera singer I should probably be before the public to-day at sixty and persist in my dramatic activities until ninety —my mother's present age. But, being a singer, I made the resolution—at twenty, mind you, three years before I made my operatic début—that I would stop singing at my apogee and grow old gracefully in caps and shawls at forty. And I carried out that firm resolution, all but the caps and shawls, by retiring before I had reached my forty-fourth birthday instead of at forty. How can one grow old gracefully to-day without being a frump? The fashions certainly do not allow one to look one's age, even when they are worn in moderation.

When I was about eleven, owing to an unfortunate turn in our financial affairs, my mother was obliged to give up one child; and since it was necessary to keep my brother in Portland, Maine, where he might continue the education that was to prepare him for his career in the navy, I was the one sent to my grandparents in Bath, Maine. My life with my grandfather and grandmother, whose idea was that love and happiness and amusement were among the least of the necessities of life, was far from a happy one. In reality, to one of my vitality and personality and strong desires, it was nothing less than a martyrdom and I fear I was a problem to them and a "handful."

My grandmother was a woman of great force of character, with a sense of humor, but a warped emotional nature. She would have made an excellent wife for a warm-hearted, understanding man with a strong hand. But she married an icicle and a problem in Euclid. My grandfather was of the black, dour Scotch type from which he descended, and extremely hard. His great interests—in another man they would have been called passions—were astronomy, mathematics in any form, and all things appertaining to politics, which were, naturally, rather limited in scope in those days, whether of town or state. During his lifetime he occupied several quite important governmental positions.

Incidentally, my grandfather's name was not Hayden at all, but Heddean, which was more the designation of an office in Scotland than a proper name; but every one called him Hayden, so to avoid confusion he had his name changed by act of legislature to the one by which he was known—a foolish step.

My grandmother had, without knowing it, what would now probably be called an artistic temperament. She was a woman of fine mind, deeply founded principles and Puritanical standards, but withal human and passionate. And passionate, alas! to the point of having actual brain storms, during which all her ideals of conduct would be thrown to the winds. I learned how unlovely such exhibitions were and determined that the same wild impulses within myself should be curbed and directed. Even at this day I prefer not to remember the moments that inspired that resolution.

Being constantly punished for small faults and mistakes as though they were crimes made me feel that a high standard of character and of behavior was an objective to strive for. This belief made me conscientious to a degree that could only be called morbid. Nevertheless, I have much for which to be grateful to my grandmother. Her severe upbringing was sane and taught me the difference between true and false pride, cultivated within me a sense of honor and self-respect, even though it implanted in my breast an unattainable ideal of conduct that in later years caused me much unnecessary self-condemnation. My entire life was colored by her influence and teaching.

A very near and dear friend of mine, a writer, Howard Sturgis, said to me one day when my career was at its height, that there was one person he would have liked to meet and that was Grandmother Hayden, who, years after her death, still had me in her clutch and reached from her very tomb to influence my life.

It was only natural that when I left the loveless atmosphere with which my grandparents surrounded themselves, the reaction, the rebound, was so enormous that I seemed unable to find sufficient outlet for my animal spirits. I turned to every kind of mischief and the perpetration of endless harmless pranks at school. It was tacitly understood, for example, that the boys and girls in a class were not to consult one another in the solution of problems, although such consultation was permitted between members of the same sex.

One day I asked if I might consult another member of my class, and upon being told "Yes" I got up out of my place and walked across the room to a boy I knew, the grandson of my grandmother's most intimate friend, and spoke to him about my problem. One could fairly feel the shock of this go through the class. But as the thing was done and there was no definite rule against it, it was allowed to pass with the exception that in my teacher's mind another black mark had been set down against me.

I never refused to take a "dare." The stonework of the schoolhouse formed, at the corner angles, a series of mounting ledges. Some one dared me to climb these to the second story. I took the dare and performed the deed, much after the manner of the modern "human fly" who awes the watching multitude.

We studied chemistry, and when I thought the lesson had been long enough I made sulphureted hydrogen and drove every one out of the building. I had no realization of my naughtiness until the principal of the school, a very fine man of intuition and intelligence and understanding (who later became an excellent lawyer and made a noteworthy career) brought it home to me. He had gone to my grandparents to speak to them of my untoward conduct: but upon beholding them in stern and solemn conclave with my two uncles, he had not been able to bring himself to put me at their mercy. He sent for me instead, and put me on my honor, and never had cause to be troubled by me afterwards.

In spite of his forbearance I was dreadfully scolded by my grandparents for the mere fact of his visit; but I never held it against him after he had made me realize my wrongdoing and explained to me that when one could lead as easily as I did one was in honor bound not to be an influence for mischief or evil. That was all that was necessary. To make me do or be the thing that was expected of me one needed only to make me understand. But from my babyhood I have always felt that I must understand.

My mother says she thinks I must have been born with an interrogation mark in my mouth. I remember her telling me when I

22

was quite a little girl, before I left China, in fact, that I must not ask "Why?" that she would not always have time to tell me why between an order and a great danger, and that I must learn to obey first and ask questions afterwards.

The greater part of this excess energy of mine was due, I am sure, to the fact that in the days of my youth girls did not play games— tennis was just beginning to be played a little by women then—and I did not have the outlet that the strenuous have to-day. My capacity for physical activity was so tremendous and so well known that many people said to me at the beginning of my career that I could always be sure of enjoying the advantage of enormous health. The truth of the matter was that from my twenty-fifth year I scarcely knew a well day or was free from pain, due to an accident which befell me about that time.

In addition to my tremendous energy I must have had a certain amount of magnetism, because at dancing school the little boys would get into the most shocking fights trying to settle which was to be my partner. As I recall, this impressed me only as a diverting phenomenon and not at all as having any personal significance. In fact, I believe I had remarkably little personal vanity—chiefly, no doubt, because of my grandmother's upbringing— except such as might be found in my determination to pull in my waist as much as possible and dress my hair in a new way every day in the inevitable silly period of adolescence.

During those childhood years I received the usual instruction in piano, but nothing ever came of it, owing to the lack of strength in my fingers. My mother had instructed me, and then when I went to my grandmother's to live, my aunt, who was a thorough musician, continued my musical education, teaching me, together with the piano, a little elementary harmony and transposition.

When I was about fifteen my mother became aware that I had the beginnings of a voice that promised to be an unusual one. Shortly after that, a cousin of an uncle by marriage on my mother's side came to Bath and heard me sing. This cousin-in-law, so to speak, Warden by name, lived in Paris, was a subscriber to the Opéra there, the Mecca of all great artists at that time, and had an ear well trained by listening to very nearly every great artist then before the public. After he had heard me sing in the Swedenborgian Church in Bath—it was "Oh, for the Wings

24

of a Dove," I remember—he said that my voice was so unusual and of such a very beautiful and touching quality that he thought it would be wicked if it were not cultivated.

The idea of opera had never occurred to me, as it had been drama that had been my lure; but now that it was suggested to me I realized that opera, after all, was simply drama with music, and that by some great good fortune my voice seemed to qualify me for this art of interpreting another character than my own, and that my beloved childhood game of "playing theater" might become a delightful grown-up occupation.

The uncle by marriage, General Thomas Hyde, whose cousinship to Mr. Warden had brought about this promising state of affairs, was much interested and persuaded my grandparents to allow me to go to my mother in Portland once a week, so that it could be seen how my voice would develop. The result of this experiment proved to be highly satisfactory.

All the time I was traveling to Portland for instruction I was studying and passing examinations at the high school in such absurd subjects for a person of my years as physical geography, political economy, chemistry, astronomy, natural history, English literature and mathematics, including higher algebra.

In the spring of 1882 my mother, having previously arranged to take me to Annapolis with her to witness my brother's graduation exercises, decided that it would not be practical for me to pass my final examinations. I was fearfully excited and delighted over the anticipated trip to Annapolis, but when I at last arrived in that gay town, fortified for the great event by a number of charming dresses my mother had had made for me, the heat and the change and the unwonted excitement made me too ill to enjoy any of it. The whole thing passed in a haze—the tea parties and dinners and ball. I had a feeling all the time of being only half there.

But later in the summer, when the North Atlantic Squadron, in which my brother was a midshipman, was due to visit Portsmouth, New Hampshire, my mother and I went to visit the aunt of the woman who afterward became my sister-in-law.

The Admiral of the Fleet at that time was "Fighting Bob" Evans. And my mother afterwards told me that he was very much taken with me. It seems that I wore at a dance on board the flagship what sounds to me now as

EMMA EAMES AT THE AGE OF SEVENTEEN

being the most hideous headgear imaginable, a little white lace bonnet trimmed with tea roses, and Admiral Evans told my mother that I looked like "peaches and cream" and that there "wasn't a rose in my bonnet that could look as fresh as my skin." Naturally I was so blissfully busy enjoying things that I was quite unconscious of my looks, which is probably one reason I appeared at my best.

All the balls and parties, combined with my passion for brass buttons, which every young girl has sooner or later, made the experience a perfectly wonderful one. Many of the evenings while we were in Portsmouth were devoted to music. I sang alone or in duets with my mother, my sister-in-law-to-be playing the violin obbligatos for us, or a naval officer called Winder, of Portsmouth, accompanying us on the flute. My last amateur spurt and my last parties!

Following this visit, in the autumn of 1882, I was sent to Boston to study. I went alone, but was quite safe in the house of two "maiden ladies" who might have stepped out of Cranford, so severe and conventional were they. I never seemed to be able to escape from the stiffest kind of Puritan atmosphere! In the same house with me were the children of William Dean Howells and some young people called Fairchild, who had fled to it as to a house of refuge from scarlet fever at home, the victim of this fever being Blair Fairchild, then a tiny child.

In that first year at Boston I studied sight reading, continued my lessons in harmony and began to hear an occasional classical concert. That winter I also saw the first electric arc lights. I came out on the street one evening, to be stunned at having these great white lights suddenly blaze in my eyes. It was quite an experience after kerosene lamps and gas.

My taking up of the study of sight reading was brought about by having B. J. Lang, the most prominent organist of his period, tell my mother, after he had heard me sing at her instigation, that I had a lovely voice, but that he could not give me a position because I did not read at sight. Humiliated at the implied rebuke, I took a little book containing two-part vocal exercises, contralto and soprano, and played one part on the piano while I sang the other at sight until, at the end of two months of this drilling, I found that I had mastered this musical trick. I had always been able to read music for the piano, of course, but music for the voice was another matter.

At the end of that winter of 1882-83 my mother arranged to join me in June, and we took most modest lodgings, as we had very, very little on which to live and our money had to go a long way.

Before she had been with me two months I had an engagement to sing in church. Alas! it proved to be a brief and inglorious one in a Baptist church in the suburbs of Boston, where I was promptly told that my services would be dispensed with henceforth, as I disgraced myself by bursting into uncontrollable laughter at the sight of half a dozen bedraggled women in black waterproofs being dipped into a tank underneath the pulpit, which had been removed for the occasion. Of course, in my later years, I came to recognize that the faith that made waterproofs and a dip in a tank as beautiful and poetic and unhumorous an experience as being immersed in a wooded stream was a wonderful faith indeed.

I was much mortified and horribly ashamed of myself after my uncontrollable outburst, and regarded my dismissal as a great tragedy. However, shortly thereafter I was engaged to sing at the Channing Church in Newton, another suburb of Boston, where I sang continuously, summer and winter, until I sailed for Europe in June, 1886.

Oh, how I remember those days, crossing the unpaved Common—a primitive Boston before all these modern improvements—in rubber boots to get to the Boston and Albany Railway Station to take a train to Newton. Twice on Sundays I made this journey and once on Friday, when I rehearsed and read for the first time the music that I was to interpret the following Sunday. In snow, in slush, in sleet, in rain! A good hardening process!

It was my good fortune to have my singing attract the attention of a number of people who became extremely valuable to me. The first of these was a great pianist; and thereby hangs an amusing tale. This artist was the blackest of black Germans, with funny twinkling eyes, a raw-boned man, tall and broad, with knotty fingers and an enormous shock of black hair and a beard that grew right up under his eyes. He was most anxious to give me piano lessons. My fingers, as I have said before, are perfectly limp, seeming to have no muscles in them, and incapable of mastering the technic of any instrument whatsoever; but still he insisted.

His studio was on the first floor of the house where he lived with his mother, and when I went there to take my first lesson—which, incidentally, was my last—he immediately burst into tears and told me he loved me—he had seen me just twice in his life—and that I must marry him at once. I received this astounding outburst with perfect calm, self-possession, and extreme disgust. With all the dignity of seventeen I drew myself up and told him coldly that I had not come here to listen to such things, but to take a piano lesson. He responded by standing before me and holding out his arms imploringly; whereupon I told him that he must let me pass, as I wished to go at once. As he did not move, I most ingloriously dodged his arms, flew by him and rushed downstairs. But before I could get to the door he was before me and on his knees in the front hall. Strategy was my next move. I made a feint as if to run upstairs again and, as he turned to follow, I dodged back, flew past him and out of the front door.

From that moment he haunted us for two or three years, constantly telling my mother she ought to make me marry him, the excuse for his frequent and unencouraged visits being that he wanted to play this and that for us. And as he was a great artist, I received a liberal musical education at his hands in spite of myself. This same musician put to music the soliloquy from "Hamlet," "To be or not to be," and having taught it to me, persuaded Edwin Booth to come and hear me sing it. I am sorry I never saw Booth again to ask him his impressions. Had he humor, they would have been worth hearing. Of course, I gave my heart and soul to the task and sang with conviction anyway. My own sense of humor could not have been developed, certainly, for me to have been able to do it. This extraordinary composition, so said the author of it, "should have been sung in the dark with the audience in grave clothes."

To him I owe some of the most beautiful moments of my life for his interpretation of Beethoven, which was profoundly emotional as well as in the finest tradition, and in which he lost himself and became the great medium.

This same musician taught me a number of the gayer and more vernal of Schubert's songs. He arranged a program to be shared between us to be played at a Wellesley College concert and afterwards at Miss Porter's school at Farmington, Connecticut. Such pretty girls in such feminine clothes as formed my audience and gave an ovation to another young girl! Mamma with her own clever hands made the dress that I wore, and charming and pretty it was in prebustle days. These young girls were most delightfully enthusiastic, and as I came down the broad staircase from the dressing room after the concert, they made a double line through which I passed while they pelted me with flowers and shouted their pleasure.

All these scenes I describe come back to me as pictures and this one is always a singularly fresh and beautiful one.

During the Boston period it was my good fortune to attract the attention of Professor Paine, of Harvard University, a composer and teacher of undisputed merit. He engaged me, with three others, to illustrate his lectures on the history of music, beginning with the Gregorian chants, which we sang from the quaint square notes, and continuing with the Italian school, the French troubadour songs, the early English, the French and German folksongs, and concluding with the last word in 1884 modern music. These lectures were given both in Boston and at Harvard. Mamma and I went frequently to Cambridge for supper, as the evening meal was called, with Mr. and Mrs. Paine to "make music." He often had some particularly interesting pupil as another guest, and it was there I met Henry Finck, with whom and whose charming wife I have always been on friendly and affectionate terms. There also I met Celia Thaxter and was thrilled with talk of the Theosophic Society and its experiments, a subject of palpitating interest to me.

I look back with tenderness to that Boston period as one of unruffled peace, although we had nothing in the way of worldly goods. However, I had only to do work that I loved and which interested me, and I had no responsibility, not even of reputation, to sustain. In the atmosphere of love with which my mother surrounded me I was blissfully happy merely in loving her and obeying and following her lead. We had few but very delightful friends, but social plans and duties were not my preoccupation. I drifted happily through all that was extraneous to my lessons and my work and was emotionally at peace.

The Boston Symphony concerts were then conducted by George Henschel, and I had the privilege of hearing many joint song recitals given by him and his gifted wife. At this same period I heard, led by him, over and over again the great works of Beethoven, Schubert, Schumann and Bach played by what was even then the most perfect orchestra imaginable, the Boston Symphony Orchestra. No pains were spared in bringing the performances of this orchestra to the utmost perfection both as regards the composition of the orchestra and its ensemble.

My first introduction to opera was when I heard "Lohengrin" with Christine Nilsson and Campanini. Nilsson was most poetic in appearance and she sang with telling conviction and much beauty of tone. But that evening, being at swords' points with Campanini over some private grievance, she had little of love or charm about her, particularly when he was on the stage with her, which was most of the time.

Before I heard any opera of the Italian school, with which the operatic education of most of my contemporaries was begun, I again heard "Lohengrin" in German and with the famous Marian Brandt as Ortrud and "Die Walküre," given by the Damrosch Opera Company under the baton of young Walter. That was a most romantic bit of operatic history.

Some Memories and Reflections

The sudden death of his father left Walter Damrosch with no other alternative than to take up the baton of his father and carry on as best he could. And because the imagination of the public was caught by seeing this handsome youth step into the breach so valiantly, and because he was a thorough musician, he was able to carry his first opera season through to a most successful conclusion. This was the beginning of his long and notable career.

It was after this that we heard Patti, my mother and I, in "Martha," by Flotow. Although she was still a comparatively young woman—in the forties—she had been singing a great many years. But her voice was entirely unimpaired. Hers was the most perfect technic imaginable, with a scale, both chromatic and diatonic, of absolute accuracy and evenness, a tone of perfect purity and of the most melting quality, a trill impeccable in intonation, whether major or minor, and such as one hears really only in nightingales, liquid, round and soft. Her crescendo was matchless, and her vocal charm was infinite. I cannot imagine more beautiful sounds than issued from that exquisite throat, nor more faultless phrasing, nor more wonderful economy of breath. Her phrases were interminable, in spite of the fact that her waist was so pinched that her ribs could not have done otherwise than cross in front, thus proving beyond the shadow of a doubt that length of breath does not depend upon the volume or freedom of the lungs, but upon the perfect pose of the voice with no waste of breath between the notes or in their production.

Later I heard Patti sing in "Sémiramide" with Scalchi as Arsace. The same vocalization was there, the same perfection of tone, the same perfection of execution, but she was swamped by Scalchi, who, in spite of her inferiority of vocal charm, was so much more satisfactory histrionically that Patti, with her curious artificial manner, became by contrast of secondary interest.

Patti had perfection of vocal art, of rhythm, of finish, of proportion, of charm, but she had the soul of a *soubrette* and in temperament was suited only to such rôles as Martha, Zerlina, and Rosina in the "Barbière." Young and utterly inexperienced as I was, I knew this even then, though I dared not voice it.

My people insisted that I study with some one who had herself studied abroad, some one other than my mother; and Miss Clara Munger, who had been a pupil in her time of Delle

Sedie, the barytone, was chosen. Miss Munger was most conscientious and careful, and brought my voice out gradually without allowing me to force it in any way. The exercises she gave me allowed my voice to develop naturally and never demanded that which was beyond my actual powers.

Then for two years, before I went to Paris, I studied the Delsarte system of gesture and devitalization with one of the greatest teachers that America has ever had in that line, Miss Annie Payson Call, who has written a great many remarkable books on this and similar subjects. She it was who taught me the necessity of absolute sincerity and clarity of thought, and how to make each muscle of my body independent, and who helped me to place my gestures so that when they were needed they were ready.

Miss Call could instantly sense—one cannot say, see or feel—the slightest contraction in any muscle that was not needed. To-day I have that same instinct, when I listen to people singing, for sensing out a fault in muscular contraction, and have often longed to tell such singers just how to overcome it. The theory of perfect singing was Patti's, the minimum of effort for the maximum of effect; not one single unnecessary muscle used; perfect articulation of the lips and tongue and absolute freedom for the column of breath from the diaphragm to the lips.

One of the first Delsarte lessons was in falling: in being taught to drop with no muscular effort at all, as the child or the drunkard or the unconscious person would fall. These never hurt themselves because they do not resist. Then once down I was taught to rise with the minimum of effort and in a devitalized condition on to a chair from the floor. This way lay grace. The hand of a child is always perfectly graceful, because there is no nervous tension. Therefore, to learn to have an entirely graceful hand, one must remove all conscious muscular effort from the hand and have the entire gesture proceed from the solar plexus, the seat of feeling. When one has this control and one's gestures are placed, one has only to feel the gesture for it to come of itself.

These exercises I continued for two winters with Miss Call, because I wished to learn the interpretative, the constructive as well as the devitalizing movements, the active as well as the passive. And I studied to such good effect that when I made my début at the Paris Opéra, I had such possession of my body and such ease of movement and freedom of gesture that it was difficult to convince Gounod that I had never acted before.

My first attempt at opera consisted in one act, the garden scene from "Faust," in which I sang Marguerite, with the pupils of Charles R. Adams, who was a celebrated singing teacher of his day in Boston, and who, not finding a satisfactory Marguerite among his pupils, asked Miss Munger if she would lend me to him.

After Mr. Henschel, Mr. Wilhelm Gericke became the director of the Boston Symphony Orchestra. He showed great interest in me, and was much interested in my voice and talent. Mr. Gericke taught me many Schubert songs. To musicians I need not tell of his sound musicianship, his taste and gift of interpretation. He was not a showy conductor, but one of profound feeling and respect for the works he interpreted, and I could not have had a better guide. Later he strongly advised my going to Paris to study under Madame Marchesi, who was at that time living in the Rue Jouffroy.

As we had no money and our family could not be called upon to help us, my mother borrowed from a friend enough to insure me a

As Marguerite in "Faust"

reasonable amount of time abroad for the perfecting of my studies, in so far as studies may be perfected, before my début.

My teacher, Miss Munger, hated the idea of my going on the operatic stage. She had been abroad and knew something of the life of the theater, and said that she had rarely seen an instance where a woman kept her integrity of character when she became a singer. Whereupon I vowed that if I had to buy my career at the expense of my character, I would have no career. It goes without saying that at that time I had not the faintest idea of what life meant in some of its phases, nor realized that I had mapped out an extremely difficult task for myself.

Before my departure for France I sang one of the sprites in Schumann's "Manfred" with the Boston Symphony Orchestra in Boston. With this same orchestra I also appeared as soloist in a number of the lesser New England towns. Then, too, I sang in a series of concerts with a quartet of wind instruments, managed by George Stewart, who became a successful manager later and has now retired. The other soloist at these concerts was Leopold Lichtenberg, who was about my age and had a certain air of poetry about him.

Some Memories and Reflections

Although I had a few friends whom I saw occasionally, I had begun, even in Boston, the life of isolation and absorption in my work which did not end until 1909. But those early American years were very, very happy ones, because they came before I had learned responsibility and the limitations of physical and nervous strength, before my financial indebtedness was a constant weight upon me, and before I had a reputation to maintain in the musical world.

We sailed from Boston on one of the best Cunarders then plying between Boston and Liverpool, a steamer that would not even be considered in the same breath with passenger traffic to-day. But to the young and enthusiastic girl, standing wide eyed and oh, so earnest, watching the shore line fade and vowing to accomplish the best work of which she was capable, even though it meant the immolation of self upon the altar of her career, it was a dream come true and not a ridiculous cockleshell riding the waves and carrying her, had she but known it, to a glory she had not visioned even in her wildest dreams.

II

AFTER a highly unpleasant journey from Boston in our cockleshell Cunarder, we went to the Charing Cross Hotel in London. Here we were shown into an enormous old-fashioned bedroom, chiefly occupied by a huge double bed with a canopy that might easily have been taken out of *Pickwick Papers*. I had a curious feeling of having been there before, and was at home immediately in the coziness and real comfort of these typically English surroundings.

As we were on our way to Paris, our stay in London was necessarily brief. We had, however, the opportunity, while there, of lunching at the Royal Court, House of Lords, with my uncle's cousin, the Hon. Mrs. William Carrington, whose husband was equerry to either the Queen or the Prince of Wales, I do not recall which. The other event of our London visit was witnessing the trooping of the colors at Whitehall. After that we sped on to Paris.

Upon our arrival in Paris we went direct to Neuilly to a small pension charmingly situated

43

in the Avenue du Roule and having its own garden. Here rooms had been engaged for us by Philip Hale, now a Boston critic, but at that time a student of the organ under Guilmant. Philip kept in his rooms a pedal piano at which he worked with great constancy and determination. His wife, whose health, undermined by the food and living conditions in Germany, had compelled her to give up her career as a pianist, was with him. They were a most interesting and enthusiastic young couple.

Unfortunately this pension, although on the same side of Paris, was at a great distance from the Rue Jouffroy, where lived Mathilde Graumann of Frankfort, otherwise Madame Marchesi of Paris; and going to a lesson with this famous teacher was like undertaking a journey to another land.

We went to see Madame Marchesi at once upon our arrival to learn whether she would accept me as a pupil. I sang for her with fear and trembling, and carefully avoided telling her that I had ever sung a note in public, lest she expect too much of me. Alas, the modesty that handicapped me in those days is quite absent from many of the young aspirants I have encountered since.

SOME MEMORIES AND REFLECTIONS

Madame Marchesi was not able to give me lessons at once, but she accepted me definitely as a pupil and told me to come to her upon her return from her vacation in the autumn. She advised me to go to some quiet place and rest in the meantime, and not attempt to sing. After this important interview my mother and I went directly to Bayreuth to hear the music festival. The Bayreuth trip had been planned by Mamma and Mr. Gericke and it was he who engaged for us the room and the places for the four performances: two of "Parsifal" and two of "Tristan and Isolde." Before we left Boston, therefore, he had passed many hours with us analyzing and explaining both operas to us, musically and dramatically. It is easy to see that the influence of that period in Boston gave me my musical direction, if one may say so, although it was my natural bent that made me love all that came to me thus, and absorb it. It was a peaceful and beautiful period and an unhurried one; and had I foreseen all the emotions and cataclysms in my future life, I should have turned my back on the Boston of those days with even greater reluctance.

Curiously enough, nothing whatsoever of

that journey to Bayreuth impressed itself upon my memory until we had passed Munich. Then, Munich having packed the little train with Germans, festival bound, I witnessed a little scene, all too indicative of the difference in the status of Teutonic and American womankind, that I never could forget. A pale, fragile little woman stood between her obese, overfed husband and the window, fan in hand, protecting her noble lord and master from the cinders and heat. Needless to say, being newly from America where woman is queen, I was perfectly horrified and indignant and shocked.

Mr. Gericke, who was vacationing in Europe between seasons of the Boston Symphony Orchestra, had been kind enough to engage for us the only available kind of room to be had in Bayreuth in those days, a room in a private house. It turned out to be a huge affair with dormer windows, and the inevitable two little German beds with their funny eiderdown comfortables, buttoned into sheets, which fell off on to the floor constantly. I am certain that it would take at least a lifetime, reënforced by the atavism of countless previous lives, to be able to learn to manipulate such a coverlet. This lodging was in the house of a school

46

master and below us were his quarters and the
school—a boys' school.

It was my first glimpse of a German village
and German life. And it all struck me as
being most charming, simple and unaffected,
as indeed it was in that long ago when the people who made the pilgrimage to Bayreuth were
idealists and real music lovers.

Our party numbered seven people. It included my mother and myself, Mr. Gericke,
two young men, Benjamin Gilman and Alan
Marquand, who were friends of ours, and
Henry L. Higginson, the patron of the Boston Symphony Orchestra, as well as his niece,
now Mrs. Graeme Haughton, who is still
one of my nearest and dearest friends. We
sat near one another in the auditorium and
had our little bite between the acts together.
That bite consisted of sausage and black
bread and cheese and beer, the sort of snack
the Germans took between the acts to forestall faintness.

How different this all was from the later
Bayreuth! The Bayreuth of 1897, which
saw my next visit, was pandemonium. Great
restaurants crowded with chattering sight-
seers; people without understanding or reverence, intent upon the latest fad—*that* was the

Beyreuth Cosima Wagner built when Wagner
and Liszt were no longer there to stop her and
she could give free rein to her commercial instincts.

But at the time of our first visit in the early
eighties the glory of Bayreuth had not become
tarnished. Liszt was still living; but afterwards he was taken ill at the performance of
"Tristan" and shortly after died. Frau Cosima
had not been allowed to put her finger in the
festival pie. Wagner had not been long dead,
and the musical and dramatic seeds he had
sown were still bearing fruit in the care of the
leaders he had trained, the two greatest being
Mottl and Levy. Even Anton Seidl, first
among the master conductors of orchestra and
opera of the German and classic school, was in
a secondary position under these older men.
To attend one of the performances was like assisting at a religious rite, the singers were so
completely forgetful of self and so utterly absorbed in bringing out with reverence the
beauty of the music drama.

We heard two performances of "Tristan"—
one with Materna and the other with Sucher
as "Isolde"—in which Vogl was Tristan.
Then we attended two performances of "Parsifal" with Materna and Malten alternating in

the rôle of Kundry, the latter at that time being comparatively young. Scaria sang the rôle of Gurnemanz and Reichman that of Amfortas. In a whole lifetime of music I have never experienced anything so marvelous, so unsurpassable in emotional and religious appeal as these performances. The singers so completely lost themselves in the characters they portrayed that one ceased to think of them as other than the personages of the music drama. What more wonderful example of selflessness in one's art could be asked!

One evening, at the conclusion of a performance of "Parsifal," Materna invited our party to go with her to a small beer cellar, where she opened a barrel of wine for the crowding enthusiasts who were waiting to drink her health. That low-ceilinged, arched cellar, the mass of excited, eager faces, the big woman with her amiable face smiling at the deafening "Hochs!" shouted in her honor, I shall never forget. It was my first glimpse of the delightful madness that is born of music.

Mr. Higginson begged my mother, during our Bayreuth visit, to call upon him in the future if more funds were needed to further my career; and later this my mother did. When I paid my indebtedness to him the first year I sang in America, seven years later, he told me that up to that time I was the only one among the aspiring young musicians and singers he had helped who had ever returned the money loaned them.

While we were in Bayreuth we made a brief excursion to Nürnberg. Nürnberg in the early eighties boasted of few visitors and no "trippers." Therefore my first European sightseeing was done under ideal conditions and we bore away with us memories of the quaint old town quite unmarred by the crowds one sees to-day herded along by a shouting guide and hardly realizing what they are seeing through the jumble of overcrowded impressions and information. There was only one hotel in the place, which was on the river bank. It was small, as inconvenient as possible, but very clean and picturesque.

After our Nürnberg jaunt we returned to Paris and devoted the time remaining to becoming acquainted with the beauties of that lovely city and its surroundings.

In September Madame Marchesi returned to Paris and the autumn work with her began.

Madame Marchesi—Mathilde Graumann of Frankfort—wife of the Marchese Salvatore

Some Memories and Reflections

Castrone de la Rajata (a Sicilian by birth and for a short period a professional singer) was the ideal Prussian drill master, a woman of much character and one to gain great ascendancy over her pupils. A thorough musician, she was an indefatigable worker. Her school was an example of discipline, order and organization. She herself, at her piano by nine in the morning every week day, was always perfectly and rather richly dressed and with never a hair out of place. In the beginning we were classed all together and each had daily vocalises for a month, a fifteen-minute lesson in class, and so on until we went through successive stages into the opera class in the afternoon. The lesson, however, always began with a few vocalises directed all in the same way irrespective of personal idiosyncrasies.

Madame Marchesi trained the voice to have three distinct registers, instead of one perfectly even scale, in which the tones of each register melt into the tones of the next as do the colors in a prism, which is the only logical way of singing. She believed, too, that a woman should not pronounce words above F in the medium, while I always felt that if a man could pronounce words on the highest notes in his voice, why could not a woman? Owing to this conviction of hers, the voices of her pupils, such as Gerster's, gave in their upper register the impression of ventriloquism, and sounded as though their owners had been taught to sing with a dropped larynx, which was indeed what we were told to do. Madame Marchesi fortunately did not attempt to change my natural singing method, and as my voice was a healthy one, she did it no harm, but neither did she give me that absolute vocal security which I was to gain for myself later. She had intelligence and the real German efficiency, but no intuition. She had a head for business which, with her excellent musicianship, gave her the position she occupied for so many years—that of owner, manager and teacher of the greatest school of her day.

She surrounded herself with the best lieutenants obtainable—teachers of Italian, of French and of "deportment," and as accompanists, *chefs de chant,* or coaches, of the Opéra—such men as afterwards became orchestra leaders of the second category. One exception I must make is the first professor of "deportment." He was an antiquated little Frenchman named Petipa, formerly a ballet dancer and instructor. He had been a contemporary of Taglioni and had danced with her, had even composed a ballet for her, and had been a celebrity in his day.

The steps he made us take, the little bows, and the instruction as to how to enter and leave a room, how to greet a hostess on arriving, or one's own guest, the exercises he taught us in the practice of equilibrium even if embarrassed by a sudden movement on the part of another—were of the most primitive. No other technic was taught us in this way, and with my remembrance of Miss Call fresh in my mind, I was intensely amused.

I had not, however, spoken to Madame Marchesi of my study with Miss Call any more than of my former public appearances. There was nothing to be gained by doing so, as I had only to prove later when opportunity should arise that they had been of use. One can easily see how such a "professor of deportment" seemed sufficient to Madame Marchesi who told us we must not make any gestures while singing, but only between the phrases, in order not to disturb the tone. She had not yet "caught up" with Wagner. I wonder what she would have thought of the gymnastics of the present-day opera singers of which some, however, do most decidedly "disturb the tone"!

She gave *auditions d'élèves*, or pupils' concerts, each year, at which we sang alone and together. Of one thing I *am* absolutely convinced, as I force my mind to bring back that period—that she did not have the faintest idea of my talent or what I had in me.

I was docile and respectful and obeyed all her directions and, as Victor Wilder (a great French critic) hoped, "found myself" later, when success immediate and overpowering allowed me to dare to believe I had something worth saying and giving in myself.

After gentle little Petipa, the "teacher of deportment," we were placed in the hands of M. Pluque, the head "mime" of the opera and head director of the ballet, or what was called a *régisseur*.

M. Pluque was a man of understanding. He not only could tell you what to do, but he was able to recognize individuality and knew how to develop it. If he saw something original in your interpretation, he did not resent its presence because, perchance, he had not suggested it, but instead was pleased, and helped you by constructive criticism to make it convincing. I could not resist the temptation to discuss the appropriateness of any gesture I felt was inconsistent with the character I was portraying as I conceived it.

Some Memories and Reflections

Singing was always to me of secondary interest to that of acting and interpreting. As far as it was possible for me, I made myself mistress of the technic of singing, in order not to be preoccupied with vocal production. M. Pluque at last ended by allowing me to make my own gestures, only criticizing them technically—as to breadth and direction, in regard to my position on the stage, and their effectiveness.

All was tradition on the French stage in those days, which meant not only traditions of style and good taste, but the engrafting of others' limitations on to one's own, as well as imitating another's qualities and stifling one's own. A divine school for mediocrity! M. Pluque had the good sense, however, to give me much latitude in everything I studied with him, and was artist enough to like the originality of ideas I showed.

Madame Marchesi had the energy not only to teach all day, but also to give occasional "at homes" with music to which a select few of her pupils were invited. At one of these I heard the great professor Diémer play. He was professor of the piano at the Conservatoire, with an impeccable technic which he had the gift of imparting to his pupils. His interpretations, however, were so shallow and meaningless that I marveled at the ovation he received, and, in fact, that his playing always elicited. It was mere tinkling, or so it seemed to me, brought up as I was in an austerely classical school of interpretation.

I also heard the famous Ristori recite at one of these "musicales." All recitations, except comic ones, give me a feeling of embarrassment, "as though the performer were one's relation." She was no longer young, and with that drawing-room background her performance was stripped of all glamour and gave me the impression of ranting. I was really sorry to have heard her. Her diction doubtless was perfect, and it was a privilege to have had such an opportunity; but when does the younger generation appreciate its predecessors unless impelled by their actual genius? As my grandmother (here she is again!) so often said: "One should not outstay one's welcome."

Madame Marchesi assumed the attitude of being above financial considerations. However, on her piano in the music room she kept a vase into which we were supposed adroitly to place on a certain date—and in advance—our monthly fee. She, of course, did not appear to notice this, but that she did notice it was proved most forcibly if any pupil neglected to place her envelope in the receptacle on the date on which it was due.

Early in my studies with Madame Marchesi my idealism received its first great shock. I had always believed that the world was large enough for everybody, even other singers; that if one had a message to give, one had enough to do in concentrating upon giving it without wasting time on professional jealousy; and that if one had a genuine gift and a real hold on the public, nothing and no one could take them from one. The thought that others might be jealous of me paralyzed and depressed me instead of causing me to rejoice, as it did many who seemed to regard it as a tribute to their art. For I had dreamed, in my innocence, of working hand in hand with other singers instead of fighting them every inch of the way.

When Madame Marchesi learned of this naïve idea of mine she was filled with horror, and immediately set about to disabuse my mind of it if possible. She was unsuccessful, unfortunately, and only future experience taught me the sordid truth of what she preached—namely, that as soon as one went into public life all other singers must be considered as enemies and that one must govern oneself accordingly and think only of protecting oneself and one's interests.

Madame Marchesi was much troubled and a little annoyed at my excessive sensitiveness to all her worldly revelations of music and musicians, as well as a certain brutality in her mode of expression. One morning in class when she saw that I was vibrating painfully to certain remarks she had made which were shocking to me, she turned to me and said abruptly: "You are much too sensitive for a career. Unless you can become hardened you will never make one."

She was quite right. The conventional career of the prima donna was not for me. Had I plunged into such a one instead of living the life of the cloister, I would never have had a career.

In October of my first year with Madame Marchesi a singer arrived who was to teach me the bitter truth of Madame Marchesi's worldly philosophy. She had a naturally placed, liquid, perfect and divinely beautiful voice. Madame Marchesi immediately began to give her private lessons for a reason that was at once vanity and professional shrewdness. Madame had a wonderful gift for train-

ing voices already placed, very real musicianship, an inexhaustible knowledge of Italian
opera and inspired invention of cadenza, but
she was not so fortunate in her way with the
undeveloped voice, although any one would
have incurred her undying enmity by saying
so. Therefore her pride made her conceal with
private lessons the fact that this brilliant new
soprano had little to learn and in truth was
well along the road to vocal sophistication before Madame ever saw her, and lacked only
taste and imagination and musical intuition.

This singer remained with Marchesi only
a year, then she made her début in Brussels in
the autumn of 1887. It would be impossible
to imagine anything lovelier than she was,
both in appearance and voice. She did not attempt to act, for she had no gift, but her
naïveté and simplicity had their own charm in
such rôles as Lakmé, Lucia, and Gilda in
"Rigoletto."

Later in the year, Madame Marchesi, having been told by her critics that she was incapable of teaching a dramatic soprano and
that all the voices that had hitherto come out
of her school, such as Gerster's and Emma
Nevada's, were purely of the lightest kind, decided that this singer should be a light or lyric

soprano and that I, young as I was, should be a dramatic soprano. This determination to have a dramatic soprano to her credit had become nothing short of an obsession with her. Therefore she began immediately to teach me, among other rôles, those that were heavier than any I ever sang at any time in all my subsequent career, such as Valentine in "Les Huguenots" and Selika in "L'Africaine." This done, she arranged a hearing for me at the Opéra and had me sing the airs from these two operas. I was immediately refused. And while I was, naturally, humiliated, I must say frankly that I was also extremely relieved, because I felt I did not have the maturity or vocal resistance to sing in operas of that caliber.

After this Madame Marchesi arranged a début for me in Brussels, and in the winter of 1887 and 1888 my mother and I settled in that city to await the great moment. While we were waiting, Mr. Gavaert, director of the Brussels Conservatory and a man of great erudition, became interested in me and thought to improve the shining hour by teaching me another rôle for which I did not have the strength, and even had I had it, my sense of humor would have prevented my singing "La Juive."

There was no sign of a début, and with the passing months my mother and I became more and more impatient. Then one day this singer, whom I have mentioned previously as my life-long instructress in operatic intrigue, with whom I had hoped to make a career side by side, unspoiled by jealousy, and whom I deeply admired, came to see us and announced: "I really should like, Emma, to know how you sing."

Thereupon she took up the opera I was studying and placed herself at the piano in order to accompany me in the most ponderous, the most empty and the most difficult air a soprano can sing, the one from "La Juive" beginning, "*Il va venir.*"

I sang it, and with so much conviction evidently that when I had finished there were tears in her eyes. And as she rose from the piano, she said: "I had no idea you could sing like that!"

Still another month passed and no word about a début. Then one day, when I went for a lesson, Mr. Gavaert said to us: "You two ladies are absolutely inexperienced in the ways of the world and the theater, and I feel that I should be very cruel and very wicked if I allowed you to continue under a delusion. This singer whom you regard as a good friend, and who is, as you know, having an enormous success, and making, as the French phrase goes, 'sunshine or rain' at will, tells you that she will resign if you are not allowed to sing. But at the same time that she is saying this to you, she is telling the directors quite the opposite. And, as she has still two more years to sing in Brussels, there is only one thing for you to do, and that is go back to Paris and look for something else to do."

Never shall I forget the blow that that revelation of a treacherous friendship was to me. It absolutely outweighed my disappointment at failing to make my début, because I felt, in spite of this miscarriage of my plans, that as long as I had my voice the future held opportunity.

We returned to Paris, and I went to Madame Marchesi, who after having made me sing all the most ponderous rôles in the world, told me that I had made my voice heavy by singing "La Juive"!

It did not take long to lighten it again, however, as I had no vocal vices, and the next move was to see where I might make my début. I had been refused at the Opéra, and had failed to make my début at the Brussels Opéra, la Monnaie. While we were pondering this problem, a strange person called Ffrench, who was recruiting singers for comic opera, wanted me to go with him. That, of course, was out of the question, not because I had any feeling of superiority about comic opera, for I have always believed that it is not what you do, but the way you do it, that counts, but because I knew I did not have the light and superficial touch necessary for success in that line.

Then, learning that Gounod was looking for a Juliette, Madame Marchesi took me to sing for him, and he declared himself much pleased, and accepted me at once as his Juliette on one condition, that I should study the entire rôle with him and under his direction. He told Madame Marchesi that she knew nothing of French traditions—which infuriated her, not, oddly enough, with him, but with me—and that he would accept me only on those terms. Nothing could have seemed more marvelous to me.

Thereafter began a series of enchanting lessons during which Gounod taught me not only Juliette but also Marguerite in "Faust," Mireille in the opera of that name, and his oratorio "Mors et Vita," as well as many of his songs, thus prolonging a delightful relationship. Numerous other things, too, I learned from him, concerning right ideals of work and the correct attitude toward one's art and public. He believed that the voice was only the canvas upon which one painted, and that one should not sing down to the public taste, for while the crowd could not always distinguish the false from the true, it would always respond to the really sincere in art. He told me, too, always to sing to the one intelligent listener, even if there were only one. I went one better than his advice, and sang to myself and my over-exacting artistic conscience.

He often sang Mozart for me, and no one could sing Mozart more beautifully. Often after our lessons he would give not only a lecture on the philosophy of art, but a little illustrated lecture on the various schools of music.

It might be well to note here that at the time I was studying Juliette with him, "Roméo et Juliette" was in the process of being transferred from the Opéra Comique to the Opéra, with a ballet newly written for the impending occasion by Gounod. Jean and Edouard de Reszke were to sing the parts of Roméo and

Photograph by Downey

As Juliet
1891

SOME MEMORIES AND REFLECTIONS

Frère Laurent respectively, Delmas was to be Père Capulet and the other rôles were to be taken by recruits from the very best secondary talent of the Opéra. Therefore it was no small honor to be considered by Gounod as worthy of singing his Juliette upon this most important occasion.

When Gounod considered me quite ready in the rôle, he not only made the appointment with the directors of the Opéra, but went with me to this "audition" and sang all the duets with me. When I had finished this memorable audition, M. Gaillard was most charming and said among many other things that my voice was fresh and beautiful and that my interpretation had poetry, but that he felt I was too young to shoulder the responsibility of introducing Juliette to the patrons of the Opéra. It was evident that I did not appeal to him personally, for all his fair words. Another grievous disappointment. The third!

Fortunately the music publisher, Heugel, became interested in my career about this time and was kind enough in the autumn of 1888 to arrange a hearing for me at the Opéra Comique. I was engaged immediately at a salary of five hundred francs a month, and signed a contract which included a clause stip-

65

ulating that my salary began the day I affixed my signature and was to be paid to me whether I sang or not.

This salary clause was the only good thing that came out of my engagement at the Opéra Comique, for Massenet, wily old fox, resolved that I should not make my début before Sybil Sanderson, of whom he was a tremendous admirer until the day of his death, especially as the great International Exhibition was coming in 1889, with its power to enhance the glory of any singer who might be appearing while it endured.

The career and life of Sybil Sanderson are too well known for me to comment upon. She was a very beautiful and greatly talented woman and afterwards became a dear and very close friend of mine. She was one of the kindest and most generous of people, incapable of meanness, and probably knew nothing of the real import of Massenet's maneuvers. It is quite certain that I did not, and my mother and I remained beautifully trusting in the face of the following events which would have aroused suspicion in any except two idiots.

First I was given "Traviata" to learn and told that I was to make my début in that. Thereupon I set myself earnestly to work to master "Traviata." This accomplished, I was told that for some mysterious reason it would be impossible for me to make my début in "Traviata," and was assigned "Mignon." I learned "Mignon" and was immediately given some reason why "Mignon" would not do for my operatic début. The last of these abortive assignments was "Les Pêcheurs de Perles."

After each of these disappointments I found myself, ridiculously enough, comforting the friends who refused to take this series of blows calmly, instead of being cheered by them. I never lost courage myself, but felt certain that some day I would have my chance.

In the month of January, 1889, a Russian impresario heard me and wanted to engage me for a three months' season in Russia, suggesting that in as much as the Opéra Comique was not using me, I could easily get a vacation. I arranged for this. The day after, I had an urgent note from the Paris Opéra asking me to come at once to see the director.

Later I learned that M. Gaillard, after refusing me had engaged an Italian singer, in whom he believed, to sing the rôle of Juliette. But Gounod refused to allow her to appear in Juliette until he had heard her in "Faust," and after hearing her in "Faust," he had declared that she was incapable of interpreting Juliette as he wished and insisted upon my being given the rôle. M. Gaillard again refused to intrust such an important performance to a débutante who might have stage fright and heaven knows what! So they effected a compromise. And it was of this compromise that M. Gaillard told me in our interview. He said that Gounod had agreed that Patti should be engaged for the first six performances, that this Italian singer should sing the next three, and that I should appear in the rôle for the remainder of my engagement, which M. Gaillard proposed to be two years.

When he had concluded I told him that I didn't see how I could, as I was engaged at the Opéra Comique. Whereupon he said, "Your engagement has only a few months more to run. Can't you get out of it?"

I then acted upon impulse and did what only a rash woman would have done. I said suddenly, "Give me that contract. I will sign it"; and immediately was the uncomfortable possessor of two operatic contracts.

Upon leaving M. Gaillard my mother and I went directly to the Opéra Comique, which was then housed in the Théâtre Sarah Bernhardt—the old Opéra Comique in Place Boildieu, which had burned, not having as yet been rebuilt—and demanded an interview with the director, M. Paravey. After great trouble and insistence on our part, M. Paravey came at last in great haste and asked, most politely: "Mademoiselle, what can I do for you?"

I answered: "I want you to send for my contract and tear it up. You have given me permission to go to Russia for a three months' vacation. By the end of those three months my engagement at the Opéra Comique will have only one month more to run. There is no reason for your keeping me tied. I want to sing. You do not let me sing. It is only fair that you send for my contract and tear it up."

His reply to this was: "I am very sorry, mademoiselle, but I have an engagement with the administrators of the theater now. Can't you come to-morrow, when we will have more time to discuss the matter?"

At this I felt myself expand morally as the genii did in coming out of the bottle. And I stood before him and said very, very quietly: "You will not leave this room. The theater administrators can wait. You will send for my contract and tear it up. Here is mine," showing him the duplicate, "and I shall do the same."

Seeing how determined I was, and probably realizing even better than I the uselessness of trying to hold me to it, he impulsively sent for my contract, tore it across and threw it into the fire. Mine followed. Thus ended my engagement with the Opéra Comique, during which I had not sung one note in public.

The next morning the announcement of my engagement at the Opéra appeared in all the papers. There was, of course, no way the Opéra Comique could prove the exact hour at which I had signed the other contract and the bird was no longer a safely imprisoned captive. Their annoyance can well be imagined.

We had a charming and ever growing circle of friends. It included a number of friends from China and their relatives, and our minister, Mr. Coolidge—the United States did not have an embassy in 1889—at whose house we were frequent guests. Perhaps one of my nearest friends, who remained so until her death, was Miss Henrietta King, the sister of Madame Waddington, whose *Memoirs* have been so widely read. Another of my closest friends was Mrs. Post, a great beauty under the last Empire, who was like a second mother to me, and whose daughter, Mrs. Francis Bacon, is still one of my intimates. Certainly no mother could have been kinder to a daughter. It was at her house that I met Madame de Osma, daughter of the Conde de Valencia, who, in later years, was to make my first visit to Spain such a happy one.

Among other pleasant remembrances of that first happy year was my association with Madame Alboni, the great contralto, of whom it was said hers was the voice of a nightingale in the body of an elephant. She had a wonderful range, the most perfectly even scale possible and great finish. She once showed me a tiny sheaf of the airs from operas which she sang at concerts and parties, and told me that she would never sing an opera in which there was one note she found difficult. These of the little sheaf she had studied for so many years that they flowed from her voice mechanically. When I contrast this handful of arias with the enormous repertoire that even opera singers are obliged to have now when they go on a concert tour, not to mention recital singers, I marvel at the difficulties the last fifty years have added to the lot of the singer.

Madame Alboni was a pupil both of Rossini and the greatest tenor of his period, Rubini. At well over sixty, and absolutely weighed down with fat, she still had complete command of her voice and could do with it as she willed. This, as well as her wonderful concentration of tone, I have always attributed to the fact that she was taught by a man, a man without prejudice in the matter of registers and lightness of sound. I have always found that if the voice is properly placed and controlled first, the lightncss will follow automatically; while if one begins with delicacy and "floating" sounds, one ends with vocal instability.

In comparison with the "stayers" Madame Alboni left the stage, both operatic and concert, very early in life. She did so, at least so she told me, because while singing she had to curb her appetite for food and could never indulge in her passion for that great national dish of her country, macaroni, in all its forms.

My mother and I dined with her frequently, and Gargantuan feasts they were. Madame Alboni and her guests made really a function of eating. Each dish, as it was brought to the table, was discussed as seriously and as lengthily as any other work of art, and with each of the many rich courses there was served a different wine. Needless to say I did more watching than eating.

Madame Alboni lived in a house built by her

on the Cours-la-Reine and now destroyed. In the period of her public life she occupied an apartment in the same building as the one in which Rossini lived, the house in the Rue de la Chaussée d'Antin, near the Grands Boulevards, which now bears a plaque to that composer's memory. And Rossini, who had hospitable instincts but who was not above cheese-paring, often used to invite his former pupil and good friend down to partake of a good solid feast of macaroni and other dishes of his country with his guests, and then invariably suggested that the party repair to Madame Alboni's for coffee and liqueurs.

This dear gluttonous soul was also an intimate friend of Alexandre Dumas, *père*, and it was at her house that I met that other Dumas, whose friendship was to prove most inspiring to me, Alexandre Dumas, *fils*. I am rather touched when I think now of the willingness of the author of *The Clemenceau Case* to waste the time over me he did. I must have amused him greatly, however, for him to have done so. Among the other things, I told him that I thought his *La Dame aux Camelias* was a book that exerted the worst possible influence on the young mind, because it made wickedness seem so beautiful.

He greeted this lofty statement with: "How do you know? Have you read it?"

I answered: "Yes; when I studied 'Traviata.' But I never shall again, as I consider it"—imagine my impertinence—"a very bad influence in that it is a glorification of immorality and presents irregularity of living in a dangerously poetic light."

He smiled and said: "Oh, yes, you will—I will prove it to you. I shall send it to you, and you will find that you cannot resist it."

I laughed, and thought little more of his boast until one day a package was brought to me, containing one of the first editions of that famous book, known in America for some unfathomable reason as *Camille*. It was beautifully bound in blue morocco with gold tooling, and fastened with a golden clasp which was locked. And there was no key!

It was irresistible. On peeping at one little corner I managed to see that he had written a long dedication to me, and I wrote in haste for the key. The key came in due course, with one of his characteristic, beautifully written and amusing letters. I unlocked the book forthwith and found the dedication beginning: "Since you ask me for the key to open this book," and followed by four pages of the most

74

masterly analysis of my character and tendencies, of which the following is an extract: "You will be sincerely loved by many men and will love also, although you neither will do so as you would wish nor be satisfied by the kind of love you will inspire. You would wish for the voice of a Malibran [whom, by the way, he adored and for whom it was said he had entertained a *grande passion*] to sing of love and the arms of a Romeo to enfold you afterwards. It is impossible. Try it!" Then came his signature and the date and in one corner at the bottom of the page was written: "To be reread in twenty years." Of course, the dedication was in French, of which the above is a free translation. He was more or less clairvoyant, and had begun our acquaintance by reading my character by my hand and physiognomy.

That, with his many valuable letters, with all Gounod's letters, the letters of many other composers and great writers, with all the scores of Gounod's operas annotated in his own hand, and all my theatrical costumes, was destroyed in a fire in which I lost all my other possessions—a disaster made possible only by the criminal carelessness of the expedition agents who undertook to send my things to

America in 1915, and that before the beginning of the submarine warfare. My four vans were put on a cargo boat over a cargo of rugs and wool which took fire from spontaneous combustion. Only *one* hold on the boat was burned —that carrying my vans.

Just before my début at the Opéra, I went to Madame Alboni at her house, in Ville d'Avray, to ask her advice about a contract offered me by the original Colonel Mapleson, who had, at various times, brought Patti to America. Colonel Mapleson wished to act as a sort of agent or adviser to me, and desired that I put myself and my career entirely in his hands.

Madame Alboni took the contract he had drawn up with this idea in mind and read it carefully. After she had finished, she returned it to me with the remark: "He has omitted only one thing, and that is that he could cut off your head if he felt like it."

It was this kindly woman who begged me not to look upon my earnings as income, but as capital, pointing out the various instances of artists of great talent and large earning capacity who, spending not wisely but too well, had had to depend upon the charity of friends in their latter years. She also taught me the rôle of Norma—another I never had occasion

76

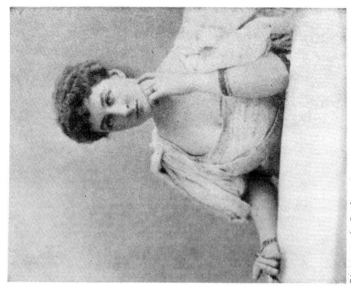

Photograph by Pettinger

1894

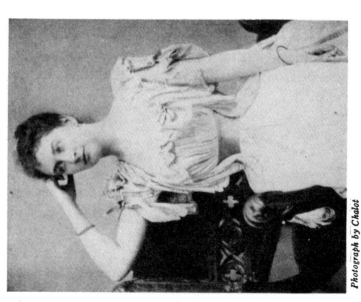

Photograph by Chalot

1890

to use—and gave me her own very beautiful cadenzas thereto. She was a most interesting *raconteuse* and told me many amusing things about her contemporaries—Rubini, Grisi, Mario, Malibran, Sonntag, and Patti in the latter's beginnings, and the Garcias, the great Spanish singers and teachers, both father and son. The former was the father of Malibran.

She said that Grisi, whom I had been taught to look upon as the greatest soprano of her period, always sang all her legato passages with a straight tone and all those requiring agility with a sort of overtone or ventriloquist note, which was, apparently, a part of the early Italian tradition for the light soprano.

It was in this same year of 1889 that I met Henry James for the first time at a large dinner party given by mutual friends, Mr. and Mrs. Edward Boit, in Paris. I found him a delightful, genial, human and humorous person, and during the next ten years I saw him often! It was with him in 1891 that I saw my first Ibsen play, "Hedda Gabler," the title rôle of which was played by Miss Elizabeth Robbins.

In later years I met him often at the home of Howard Sturgis, a dear friend who kept bachelor hall in a most delightful house called Queen's Acre at Windsor, and was himself a writer of great talent. Howard Sturgis, however, published few of his works. Of these, the two most important were *Tim*, a charming book about a rather morbid little boy at Eton, and *Belchamber*, a realistic picture of some people in the smart set in England. This last was most interesting and highly unpleasant. A Frenchwoman once said to me after reading it: "Why didn't he put in just one good little English couple to sweeten the book?"

Henry James was a delightful conversationalist, but one of those who believe that there is no such thing as a synonym. He would use only the one exact word that he felt expressed his idea. This word did not always come to him immediately, and when it failed him all talk was halted and we had to sit in solemn silence, not daring to speak or prompt him, because that upset him dreadfully, until he remembered the word he wanted. When at last he found it, one felt that it had been worth waiting for, because it always conveyed, as none other could have, the exact shade of meaning that he had had in mind. He had, by the way, a great love for dogs, and an instinctive understanding of them that would have endeared him to me had nothing else done so.

It was he who said that I was too fundamental to be happy. It was, however, that very defect or quality of which he spoke that made my art the absolute expression of my convictions or inspiration, and gave it the merit of being sincere, of expressing myself, I was going to say at first, but that is not just, for art, sincere, honest art, is selfless. This attitude of mind does not make for happiness, but is, alas! the outcome of the artistic temperament, and is what Emerson calls "divine discontent." But although it is subject to infinite suffering, the artistic temperament has its compensations in one's keen vibration to beauty in all its forms. My *Memories* so far may sound rather gloomy; therefore, I would like to add that my taste for simple pleasures, my love of nature, literature and animals, and my warm affection for my friends—few but tried—brought much that was of deep satisfaction into my life. The greatest leaven and heartener of all—a sense of humor—with an appreciation of wit, lightened a world that, with all its satisfactions and exaltations and joy of accomplishment, was too inhuman a one to fill the needs of my second self. I had a great enough wish to be happy to be willing to make happiness out of what I had; and on the other hand, my greatest joys came from my work, which, as with everything we are intended to do, possessed me utterly from 1883 until 1909. I have had a life stormy and often cataclysmal, but all the same a life containing many beautiful hours. I evolved a happy philosophy which helped me to "carry on" without being destroyed.

Not a great while before my début—in February, I believe it was—I met, at the home of some near friends, Julian Story, grandson of the great jurist judge, Joseph Story (whose *Laws on Contracts* is used even by the British Bar) and the son of William Story, the poet and sculptor.

My mother found Julian perfectly delightful, and talked with him all the evening. She was highly amused by the fact that I paid no attention to him whatsoever, and told me afterwards that had he been a poor, miserable man, ill at ease and out of place, she did not doubt that I would have devoted my whole evening to entertaining him, but since Julian happened to be both charming and distinguished, I took it upon myself to be contrary and would not even speak to him.

About two months later—after my début— when I was walking home from a tea party somewhere in the neighborhood of our apartment, I met Mr. Story face to face. He stopped, spoke delightfully of my singing, and asked if he might see me home. He did so, and came in and had a most agreeable and friendly little chat with us. He asked my mother if he might paint my portrait, and invited us to tea at his studio on an afternoon three days later.

On the day appointed we went to his studio for tea, and afterwards my mother, having an important errand to do, left me and I went on to pay a call in the neighborhood. Mr. Story, saying that he had an appointment at the same house for that afternoon, accompanied me. This was rather unusual, as in those days no young girl ever was seen alone with a young man, and I never went anywhere unchaperoned by my mother except to the houses of such intimate friends as were quite in the neighborhood.

We reached the house of our mutual appointment in due time, and as we were walking up the stairs, Mr. Story told me he loved me and asked me to marry him. This, the third time we had met!

Alas! It was Romeo and Juliet all over again. I thrust the thought of it from me at once, paid my call and rushed home overwhelmed with grief and horror. I had wanted to give myself entirely to my work, to my career, and I recognized at once that love was a hideous complication, and that this love would bring me great trouble and sorrow before I had finished with it.

My sense of responsibility had always been very great, and the debts incurred by my mother in my behalf lay heavy on my conscience. I did not feel that I could contemplate marriage until they had been paid in full. Ultimately this was discussed with Mr. Story, and he was willing to wait until such time as I could marry him, unhaunted by debt.

Julian was a man of infinite charm and grace of bearing, of distinction and education and, up to the time he met me, had never contemplated marriage. Unfortunately, we were not well mated, chiefly due to the fact, undoubtedly, that we were both too absorbed in my work and its advancement, and to his constant preoccupation not in any way to interfere with it. My success was as great a passion with him as it was with me. He said to me once that he had never known what it was to hate until he hated the enemies made by natural jealousy of my career.

It was in these first months of that momentous year of my life, that I found it necessary again to cheer up my friends about the continued delay of my début. It seemed as though those nine performances by Patti and Gaillard's Italian singer would never be finished. The only reason for this delay, however, was the repeated inability of Jean de Reszke to sing on account of throat trouble, which state of things, alas! recurred during his entire career. How many times afterwards did I pass agonized evenings singing with his substitute thrown in at the last minute! My friends, not knowing the exact terms of my contract with the Opéra, imagined that all these delays were a repetition of the Opéra Comique episode, and that in the end I would not be allowed to sing.

During this period of waiting, Miss Fanny Reid, a sister of Mrs. Paran Stevens, a very devoted friend of Massenet and a most unwise friend of Sybil Sanderson—as friends can be—rushed through the American colony begging every one not to go to hear me should my début materialize, saying it would be waste of time, as she was certain that my voice could not be heard across the footlights. When I think of her efforts, I am tempted to cover her grave with flowers. Never did any one do a débutante a better turn than she in begging people not to expect too much of me!

Some Memories and Reflections

A friend of my mother was anxious to do what he called "square the critics" before my début. The tradition was that the critics were very touchy and not likely to be amiable to those who had not done something for them beforehand.

My mother asked me what I wanted to do in the matter, and I replied, "Nothing!" I desired to know if I had any real talent, and did not wish to influence people to speak well of me, if such a thing were possible, and then go on singing in opera whether I was fitted for it or not, on the strength of their prejudiced opinion. Therefore, I came before the public unheralded, and with no influence to back me except what might have been gained from the one luncheon party given by Madame Marchesi for the critics of one or two papers, one of which, I believe, was the *Figaro*.

At last, after these trying delays and gloomy prophesies of my friends, I received word that I was to sing. It came to me in the form of a green postal card with this formal announcement on it:

Mercredi, le 13 Mars Représentation
ROMÉO ET JULIETTE

and on the other side, my name.

III

MY rehearsals in "Roméo et Juliette" consisted of a few hours' practice with Jean de Reszke for the stage business and for the duets. The orchestra I heard only from the audience at two or three performances of the nine preceding my début, which meant, of course, that I heard it from exactly the opposite direction to that from which it would come to me on the stage. I heard it, so to speak, the wrong way round, and had no orchestral rehearsal whatever.

Before the actual performance I went through every kind of mental jugglery to keep myself from being panic-stricken. I even pretended that I was Juliette, and that the audience would accept me as such and not think of my being Emma Eames at all. The immediate result of all this self-hypnotism was that I arrived at the Opéra the evening of my début in a state of apparent great calm.

Because of Gounod's faith in me, most of the noted French composers, including Saint-Saëns, Joncières, Massenet, and many others were present, possibly in their hearts expecting very little of me. But after my entrance: *"Ecoutez, c'est le son des instruments joyeux!"* the applause was like a clap of thunder. I shall never forget the sense of failure that flooded over me at that overwhelming outburst; yes, failure. I stood there on that stage and thought: "I have not been able to convince them that I *am* Juliette. Otherwise they would have kept silent. They are applauding Emma Eames, not Juliette."

It was, no doubt, a rather morbid reaction, but it must be remembered that, except for my "audition" in Brussels, my "audition" at the Opéra Comique, where I had come in contact only with directors and coaches, I had no experience of the theater and no understanding of the stage or of the psychology of audiences. I had only unattainable ideals.

I had one dreadful moment after that, just before the balcony scene. Suddenly, for no apparent reason, my voice became very small, and I remember as though it were yesterday the effort I made to get hold of myself and go on to the triumphant end of the opera.

It is interesting to note here that, thanks to Annie Payson Call and the training she had given me in the technic of acting, in America, I was so assured in my action and so mistress of my gestures that Gounod (as I have said before) found it difficult to believe I had never been upon any stage before.

It was a curious experience to go to the Opéra a nobody, and to find oneself the next day the talk of two continents. However, I was so concentrated upon what I wished to accomplish that this phenomenon had only a passing effect upon my mind.

Concerning my début, the critics were absolutely boundless in their enthusiasm and unanimous in their praise, and theirs were the last criticisms I ever read of any performance of mine. This, not because I felt myself above criticism, but because the criticism of others could not be on a line with my merciless criticism of myself, and would either obscure to me my own objective or give me a sense of haste and the feeling that I had not made my meaning understood. I did this on principle and for fundamental reasons as I did not wish to be either praised or blamed on any lines but my own, and I consistently held this attitude. These first reviews I read because I wished to see if others considered that I had the material for an operatic career, and upon concluding the last one, I knew that they did.

Following that first Juliette performance,

many reporters from leading American newspapers besieged me, demanding interviews. But I could only tell them that I knew very little, having just begun, that I really had nothing to say, for my experience could interest nobody. I suggested that if they waited a few years I might be able to tell them something worth hearing.

The first note of congratulation I received from any one, amusingly enough, was a fulsomely worded one from Massenet, who must have been in a perfect rage at seeing his good work on behalf of Sybil Sanderson at the Opéra Comique overthrown. For had I not, after all, made my début at the Opéra before Sybil's début at the Opéra Comique in "Esclarmonde," written specially for her by Massenet to show off her phenomenal high notes and her brilliant execution, as well as her great beauty and grace?

The morning after my début our sitting room at the pension was so filled with flowers that one could scarcely move about in it, and I remember I spent the whole of that morning weeping over the standard that the world had accepted as mine. I was so filled with the knowledge of my inexperience and a sense of unworthiness that I trembled with apprehen-

Photograph by Downey

AS JULIET

sion lest I be "found out" in my next opera. Therefore, when shortly after lunch the same singer who had prevented my début in Brussels came to see me and told me that I had looked perfectly beautiful and had sung perfectly false all the evening—perhaps no remark could have borne better testimony to my vocal trueness!—I immediately thought: "I wonder if I did," and was more wretched than ever. And in the face of all this I had to sing in "Roméo et Juliette" again the following evening!

In the days of my début the Opéra and its devotees were extremely distinguished. Only the men who had the entrée to the most exclusive clubs were subscribers, and only subscribers were admitted behind the scenes. Some of these were most boring, but many were survivors of what one rarely sees now, the real *grand seigneur* of the old school.

The first time I sang in "Faust," I remember in particular one, not of the *grand seigneur* variety, who stood beside me just as I was going on for the church scene and persisted in filling my ears with tales of how wonderful a certain Gabrielle Kraus had been in that scene, and how ineffaceable was her memory! It was curious that even then I was infinitely more thrilled at the idea of acting than of singing. I considered it much more of a tribute to be asked: *Vous allez jouer ce soir?* (Are you going to act to-night?) than "Are you going to sing?" Singing was to me merely a necessary adjunct to opera, and my idea was to become so perfectly mistress of my voice that I could forget it.

I made my début at the Opéra from a small pension in a street, then quite new, leading off the Avenue Victor Hugo. After my début I went to pay my respects to Madame Marchesi, and found her in the middle of a class. Once the social amenities observed, she turned to me suddenly and asked: "How did you come down here?"

I answered: "By tramway."

"What!" she exclaimed, "Mademoiselle Eames de l'Opéra, in a tramway! Do you mean to say that you haven't your private carriage?"

I said: "But I can't afford a private carriage. My friends all know what I make, and I cannot bear the thought of running into debt."

Her answer, which was most characteristic of her, was: "Well! When one is as beautiful as you are, one should be able to have everything."

And it immediately flashed over me: "What is this degrading work I am doing that such a thing should be taken for granted?"

That summer the Prince of Wales, afterwards King Edward VII, came to Paris to pay an official visit to the exhibition. He naturally, also, wished to see at the Opéra what was then a sensational "Romeo and Juliet." One evening when he was present, Miss Henrietta King—who had, of course, met His Royal Highness frequently in London, where her sister, Madame Waddington, was the wife of the French ambassador—had accompanied me to the theater, my mother being ill with one of her bad headaches. As I was dressing hastily for the second act, a knock came at my door and a voice said: "His Royal Highness, the Prince of Wales, wishes to pay his respects."

Intensely concentrated upon the business in hand and not thinking, I called: "He must wait."

Miss King, much amused, looked through the slightly open door, saw him laugh and heard him say: "Of *course* I'll wait."

And then and there began a friendship, which was one of the most deeply treasured of my life, with a man who has been accused of being incapable of having a disinterested friendship with a woman. I should have had no career in London at all had it not been for him, although at the time I did not suspect it. For I was an American and, very beautiful then—I can say it now at sixty—and was cordially disliked by certain ladies of the smart set in England, who regarded me as an absolute Puritan and an idiot because I had moral standards instead of purely social ones, and who went out of their way to hinder my career in England. This, of course, immediately enraged and disgusted the other type of English lady of whom, I am happy to say, there were a great many, and won me their partisanship as well as that of the Prince of Wales. Is it any wonder that I was always deeply grateful to those who did everything in their power to hamper my career, since it invariably brought me ten times more good than evil?

Among the various people for whom I sang at receptions and large parties after my début were Prince and Princess Radzivill and the great Alexandre Eiffel of Eiffel Tower fame. M. Eiffel proved to be an ugly, pleasant little man, distinguished by a most amiable manner.

Most of these private appearances were uneventful enough, with the exception of one at a huge party given by Chandon de Briailles, the big champagne manufacturer at Epernay, in honor of a marriage that had just taken place between the two ducal families of de Luynes and d'Uzès. During the course of the festivities I was offered champagne and, never having tasted wine, I refused it, to the enormous amusement of its famous makers.

One day, after I had been singing publicly for a number of months, one of the most brilliant of the Paris critics, Victor Wilder, a noted opera librettist and a great writer, said to me: "I hope to live to see you find yourself and forget all the vocal conventions you have been taught."

His remark made a great impression on me. It not only made me realize that I was not alone in recognizing what must be remedied, but it strengthened me in my resolve not to allow myself to be turned aside from the pursuit of my ideals by hackneyed tradition. In fact, my refusal ever to read any review—with the exception of those of my first night—of any performance of mine in the entire course of my career was based upon this resolution.

My grandmother once told me that I had eyes like a pig, a nose like the prow of a ship, and a receding chin, and that no one would ever love me for my looks—a good antidote for vanity. And as a result, I was never afterwards able to disabuse myself entirely of this impression.

Her fault finding, while it gave me a capacity for endurance that certainly helped me in my career, instilled in me at the same time so many doubts of myself, and so much belief in the infallibility and rights of others, that when certain crises arose later, not only my health, but my very reason, was endangered.

During the whole of my career there was among my friends only one critic, the music critic, Henry T. Finck. Mr. Finck was studying with Professor J. K. Paine at Harvard, at the same time that I was illustrating Mr. Paine's lectures there, and we often met at the home of the Paines, whom, as I have previously said, I knew very well. On our first trip to Beyreuth, chance made Mr. Finck a fellow pilgrim, and our friendship was thus sealed. Not the least delightful part of it was that I had and have a great affection for his perfectly charming wife.

Few, if any, of the critics, however, seemed to be aware of the fact that I did not read their reviews. After I had been singing at the Metropolitan for a number of years I was told, one evening during the performance, that Hermann Kline, the English critic, was in the wings asking to speak to me. He immediately launched into profuse praises of my singing, and to my bewilderment, began to revile himself for having written so many harsh things of me in London, and implored me to forgive him. I hastened to reassure him, but I have often wondered how much solace he got out of my telling him that I had nothing to forgive, and had never been hurt because I had never read anything he had ever written of me.

With my psychology, the line I took in the matter of the music commentators was the only possible one for me. Not being confused by many and divergent opinions, I was able, both histrionically and vocally, to avoid the stale and the stereotyped. For instance, one day I realized that I had fallen into the habit, so dear to Jean de Reszke and Caruso, who abused it to a fault, of using too often a portamento effect. I went home and got out all my scores, and went through them, eliminating every portamento except those that were absolutely indispensable.

During 1889 I sang Juliette on an average of ten times a month, and did not know the meaning of fatigue. In the winter of 1889-90

I added Marguerite to my repertoire. In the summer of 1890 my mother decided that our vacation should be spent in London. Our holiday began by our being met on the platform of Charing Cross Station by an acquaintance who begged me to save the evening for Lady Ardilaun by singing at a party which the latter was giving in Carlton House Terrace. It seemed that the prima donna—hateful word—upon whom Lady Ardilaun had been counting had disappointed her, and I was besought to take her place.

I had not gone prepared to sing at all; furthermore, I had been prostrated by seasickness on the loathsome Channel boat and felt utterly unfit to do anything except go to bed. But as the clarion call to battle galvanizes the charger into action, so did this demand upon my voice brace me. When the evening came I was in splendid condition and sang as well as I had ever done in my short career. My mother always used to call me her "emergency girl" because whenever I had to overcome difficulties or put up a big fight my voice was not only ready, but I sang the better for the odds being against me.

Sharing the program with me at that party was the same Mrs. Henschel whom I had heard in recital with her husband so often in Boston. Five years before she had told me, after an "audition," that it was absurd for me to consider a career in opera; that I was much too old to begin. I wondered that evening if she remembered the incident as she saw the honors of the occasion go to me. In my heart, I really thought she sang better than I did in spite of my greater success.

Oscar Wilde was one of the guests that night. It was my only glimpse of him, since I was too young to have seen him in his Bunthorne period in America.

Except for those two incidents, however, the party passed in more or less of a haze before me. But afterwards I was very glad to have made the effort, because it won for me a true and treasured friend in Lady Ardilaun, who remained so until the circumstances of our lives obliged us to lose sight of one another.

After this event, we went to Windsor to spend the day with friends, and in the afternoon Mr. Story, who had followed us to England, wanted to show me certain parts of Windsor Forest, and suggested that we should go for a drive in a dogcart. At the last moment, my mother decided that she would not allow me to go alone, and, rather than give up the expedition, I resigned my place in the dog-cart to her and mounted the seat behind. It was one of the fashionable high dogcarts of the period.

On the return drive Mr. Story got down to take a stone out of one of the horse's hoofs, and being rather cramped from balancing on the back seat, I got down likewise. The stone removed and the horse made comfortable again, I started to climb back into my place. As I did so, my mother inadvertently jerked the reins, and I lost my balance and fell from the great height of the cart flat on to my back in the road. I was stunned, but apparently not disabled or unduly affected by the fall and subsequent shock. But in a very short time I began to be inconvenienced and, in spite of my vigorous constitution and powers of recupera-tion, from that time until the end of my career I had to take infinite care of myself in order to be able to pursue my work at all.

The last year of my engagement at the Opéra was more or less of a nightmare. Upon my return from England the director told me that they were planning a revival of "Hamlet" that season, and asked me if I would sing Ophelia. I replied that while I could sing it, if necessary, I did not consider the color, quality or volume of my voice in the least suited to the music of the rôle. Whereupon M. Gaillard mentioned the singer who had prevented my début in Brussels and asked me what I thought of her interpretation of it. I told him truthfully that I had heard her sing it, and that she not only sang, but looked the part to perfection, and I believed it would be impossible to find any one who could do it more beautifully. He then asked me if I had any objection to their engaging her, and I said "No."

M. Gaillard had offered me a weapon which I refused. I have always been suspicious of the good that comes of evil or revenge. In fact, the one great superstition of my life grew out of my observation of the curious way the repeated attempts of the singer in question to hurt me always brought me luck, and never in all my career, when the opportunity was given me—and it frequently was—to harm her or others, did I take advantage of it.

I might add that I always felt that, if I had to meet rivalry with such methods, it would indicate that I had nothing worth while of my own to give. Not that I felt myself superior to other singers or thought that I sang better, but I believed that sincerity and personal worth should hold their own without the aids of cunning and intrigue.

The first thing that she did upon her arrival in Paris was to proceed to alienate Madame Marchesi, upon whom she believed me vocally dependent. This she accomplished by leading Madame Marchesi to believe that I was unfaithful to her. The method used to convince her was the bringing to her notice of articles I had neither written nor even read, but the authorship of which was attributed to me.

There was nothing that I could do to avoid the result of these maneuvers. Madame was not the type to remember that there are always two sides to every story. Baron Haussmann, whom we knew intimately, was entirely in sympathy with me in the matter, but realized as I did that nothing could be done.

At last the inevitable happened, and Madame Marchesi sent me word that since I had been utterly disloyal to her she never wished to see me again, nor did she care to listen to any defence that I might be ready to make with the idea of appeasing her. I took her at her word, and she never did see me again—at least, not for many years. The summer I sang "Aïda" for the first time in London (in which opera she heard me), I met her there at the home of an acquaintance. At this reunion she overwhelmed me with her admiration for my voice and for my art.

After the Marchesi episode, the singer who had been instrumental in upsetting the relations in this connection, now turned her attention to Gounod, so Baron Haussmann told me, and begged him to take Juliette away from me and give it to her. But here she was not so successful, the only result being that it made my true friend, Gounod, infinitely more devoted to my cause than before.

Incidentally, Baron Haussmann was the prefect who planned the streets of modern Paris. It is amazing to note that, years before the "horseless carriage," his plans anticipated its needs and were made to relieve the then undreamed-of traffic congestion of the present day. He was often attacked by those who believed that this opening out and changing of the Paris streets was putting a fortune into his pocket, and he often said to me sadly: "Let them wait until I am dead; when I die a poor man, as I shall, they will realize that I did not feather my own nest."

Another famous man who was criticized brutally on every occasion, but who was not at all saddened by it, as was Baron Haussmann, was de Blowitz, the well-known correspondent of the *London Times,* too familiar a figure in the latter part of the nineteenth century to need any identification. He was a most amusing man, enjoyed a joke at his own expense, and had the full courage of his convictions. The story is told of him that, on one occasion at the play, in passing in and out during the entr'actes he was obliged to incommode two ladies who did not take this disturbance philosophically. The last time he passed them their grumblings became so loud that he was unable to ignore them, and turning towards them courteously, he said: "Ladies, you should pity, and not blame me. My corpulence can only bother you for a moment, while I am obliged to bear with it all the time!"

One day de Blowitz said to me: "I haven't been attacked for a whole week. I must be failing. I must hurry up and do something that will draw their fire!"

In my last strenuous year at the Opéra I created two new rôles: that of the heroine in "Zaïre," by Véronge de la Nux, and that of Colombe in "Ascanio," by Saint-Saëns. There is no doubt in my mind that I was less effective in this second year than in my first, and that I

Photograph by Benque

"ZAIRE" BY VÉRONGE DE LA NUX
"CREATION" PARIS OPERA
1890

sang less well, not only on account of the constant intrigue which I encountered at the Opéra, but also because of personal trouble and anxiety.

I had been engaged to sing in London the following spring, that of 1891, and just before I left to fill that engagement Maurice Grau came to me and asked me to come to America the next winter and make one of a company he was then forming, that was to include the de Reszkes, Lili Lehmann, Marie Van Zandt, Emma Alboni, Scalchi and others. He told me he was intending to present "Roméo et Juliette," "Lohengrin" and various other operas of Jean's repertoire and mine. I begged him, however, to wait until after the London season before asking me to sign any contract. I told him that I felt that I had not been doing myself justice that last year in Paris—I had been too unhappy for many reasons to have the heart for work—and that I believed I could make better terms with him after "my success in London." He was much amused and asked me what made me think I was going to have "success in London."

The truth was, I knew intuitively that a change of environment and public would stimulate me, help me to find myself again, and forget the nightmare of that last year in Paris. I made my London début in the rôle of Marguerite in "Faust" on the seventh of April, 1891, and my rash prediction as to success was more than realized. Upon this occasion Faust was sung by a tenor called Perotti and Mephistopheles by Victor Maurel, a rôle of which he gave an interesting interpretation, but which was not particularly well suited to his voice.

That season my mother, who was very fond of society, accepted a great many invitations for us, and I, being too young to be greatly affected by external impressions and not knowing the meaning of fatigue, enjoyed every minute of the social, as well as the professional, side of my life.

One of our invitations came from an American woman bearing one of the great titles in England, the Duchess of Manchester, *née* Yznaga, at the command of the Princess of Wales, who had expressed the desire to meet me. The beauty of the Princess of Wales in the days before she became Queen Alexandra was too great, too lovely for adequate description. Upon meeting me she evinced herself most interested, but after a few preliminary compliments on my singing, her curiosity seemed to center on the question of whether or not I wore stays! My suppleness evidently intrigued her, as, in reality, I wore only the merest excuse for a corset.

Another "command" party, one given by Alfred de Rothschild, at which I sang, had a most interesting inception, of which, at the time, I was not aware. Before I had come to London, a lady of title, and of most distinguished family, holding a very high position at court—and incidentally a friend of the arch enemy who had prevented my début in Brussels!—had gone from one important person to another begging them all to show me no attentions or do anything to further my interests. Among the many whose allegiance she had succeeded in winning was Alfred de Rothschild, one of the most influential men at Covent Garden. This reached the ears of the Prince of Wales, and had the effect of a boomerang as far as the enemy was concerned. The Prince felt that out of very justice he must befriend me, and the "command" party at Alfred de Rothschild's followed, at which were present many bearing some of the most distinguished names in England at that day, when a title presupposed both lineage and breeding. And to further signify his attitude in the matter, the Prince of Wales after the concert took me down to supper—at which he devoured six plover's eggs among other things—before all those who should have had precedence. In after years I realized that it was almost as if he had told my enemies to keep hands off. I have no doubt that this gracious act of his made all the difference in the world to my career in England. And it was most characteristic of the Prince that no suggestion of what he had done for me ever came to me from him.

It was during this period that I became filled with disgust at that small set in England—fortunately very small—called in those days "the smart set," or the "Prince of Wales's set," and was horrified to hear the discussions that took place over the various lovers of the different ladies of this set.

I was not a prude, but I was both fastidious and chaste in mind, and such cheapness shocked me unspeakably. I used to call them "banderlog" people after those in Kipling's *Jungle Book,* because they fouled everything holy and misused everything beautiful. Theirs was the type of which Michael Arlen writes so revealingly to-day. They were pagans, as one of them himself said, and, I am perfectly convinced, liked me as little as I liked them.

Later, when Mr. Story became my husband, he used to tell me that, while my censorious attitude toward this very small section of British society—to which, as I have said, I was probably as unwelcome as it was to me!—did great credit to my heart and character, it was most provincial and bourgeois to display it. And he often reproached me bitterly for my inability to conceal my disapproval of this set and their ways. At last I solved an embarrassing problem by refusing to go to those places where my moral and social code would appear to my disadvantage.

The Countess of Warwick, a woman of great beauty both of face and figure, but with a rather disconcerted and unamiable expression, whom I met in the Prince of Wales's set, was distinctly of them, but had an air at once so aloof, so insolent and so proud, that it was a delight to look at her as one of a type. All the women of the "banderlog" adopted the attitude that they were above all moral laws and recognized only social ones.

However, quite apart from the "smart set," I was able to make a few deeply treasured friends in England, whom I saw as often as my work permitted. I must admit, however, that I had little opportunity of seeing any one, and little time for diversions of any kind. For if my professional life seemed to me impossible when away from its activities, on the other hand, a normal life seemed to me equally unnatural in the middle of an opera season. Strangely enough, I rarely went to the opera, but for relaxation turned to the theater and orchestral or instrumental concerts of all kinds, apparently wishing to take my drama and my music in separate doses. One of my forms of amusement was visiting the zoölogical gardens of whatever city I happened to be staying in, led there by my great love of animals. For my walks and exercise, I went to the zoo, and my acquaintances there far outnumbered my human ones. These interests and my intense love of reading gave me a very full life, and I did not realize what an isolated one it was until I stopped singing.

After I had sung Marguerite that first year in London, I sang Elsa in "Lohengrin," and "Mireille," and on the very last evening of the season Desdemona in "Othello." Desdemona, a rôle I had long coveted, had been promised me at the beginning of the season, but Albani had been scheduled for a number of performances in it, and my opportunity to sing it did not come until the last moment. And even then the performance was threatened by the differences between Jean de Reszke and Victor Maurel, and was only saved by Dufriche (afterwards well known in minor rôles in America and as assistant stage manager at the Metropolitan) stepping into the breach and singing the rôle of Iago.

On the very day of this "Othello" performance my personal affairs came to a climax. My mother, after having at first approved of my engagement to Mr. Story, now opposed it, and during the whole of the last troubled year, opposed it violently. This was due to no fault in Mr. Story's attitude towards her—he could not have been more courteous or considerate of her—but to some unknown reason or reasons of her own which may have been most sound. But unfortunately for us both, her manner throughout the whole affair was just the one best calculated to throw any girl who was very much in love.and very loyal, straight into the arms of her fiancé. At one time, however, we did manage to effect, after many stormy sessions, what appeared to be a compromise. I agreed after the signing of my contract for the American season with Mr.

Grau, to wait two years, or until my debts were paid (as I had promised), before marrying Mr. Story, on the one condition that my mother did not oppose his going to America at the same time we did.

But even this concession did not clear the atmosphere, and, to make a long story short, the situation became so tense by the end of the London season that at last I consented to going to the Registrar's office the day after the Desdemona performance and being married without my mother's consent, on the condition that I might return immediately after the ceremony and tell her. I wanted no suggestion of a runaway match.

The night of the "Othello" performance—which was the night before my marriage—the Prince of Wales, who was present at all my London performances, came to see me during an entr'acte, and I confided my plans to him. The Prince was the only outsider who knew of the impending event, with the exception of our witnesses and my devoted friend, Miss Fetridge. I had asked the latter to come to the house at which we were staying so as to be near Mamma.

The Prince seemed greatly interested and wanted to know all the particulars, and the

As Desdemona in "Otello"

first letter of congratulation and the first present—a handsome tourmaline brooch elaborately set with diamonds—that I received after my marriage, came from him.

My husband brought me back home directly from the Registrar's. Upon learning of my marriage at the Registrar's my mother was irreconcilable, and it was not until fate brought us together again nine months later that we reached any sort of an understanding.

Following our interview with Mamma I went down to Windsor to stay with a Miss Van der Weyer, the daughter of the Dutch Minister to England and a treasured friend of Queen Victoria's. His children were childhood friends of the royal children.

Here I awaited the second and final ceremony in the church, hoping that my mother would become sufficiently reconciled to attend what we considered the real marriage. It must be confessed that it was only through influence that we were able to have this second wedding and prevail upon the Vicar of Bray to officiate, for only one ceremony is looked upon as admissible in England, and the whole affair was most irregular. However, we managed, and three days after our marriage at the Registrar's office, Mr. Story came

III

down from London, and we were married for the second time, at Bray Church.

We went to Oxford for our wedding journey, and here we were pursued by a newspaper reporter who had somehow got wind of the whole affair. We caught a glimpse of him on the day of our arrival and did our best to avoid him. But at midnight we were awakened by the hotel porter pounding on the door and saying to my husband: "There is a gentleman downstairs who has been inquiring for you all day and seems to know you. He has just been brought in intoxicated by two men of the town. What shall we do with him?"

You can well imagine where Mr. Story told them to take him!

After a week at Oxford, we spent a few days with a friend of ours, Gery Cullum, at Hardwick House, his beautiful place near Bury St. Edmunds. Gery Milner Gibson was the son of the man who inaugurated the penny post in England, but upon inheriting Hardwick House he had been obliged to add the name of his maternal grandmother to his own, making it Gery Milner Gibson Cullum.

Bury St. Edmunds, where lie the relics of the martyred king, Edmund of East Anglia, who was killed by the arrows of the Danes in 870, will be remembered as the place immortalized by Dickens in *Pickwick Papers:* and during our stay at Hardwick House—which, by the way, has just fallen to the Crown in default of heirs—we went to the famous Angel Inn and found it little changed from the days of our delightful Pickwick.

Our wedding journey next took us to Paris, to the little house with the large studio and charming garden at 7 Place des États Unis, on which site we later built the delightful house which stands there to-day, but which I no longer own.

It was to the little house with the garden, however, that Whistler often came during the early years of my married life. The first time he ever dined with us he was an hour late. Planning on having dinner served at eight-fifteen, I had asked him to come at eight o'clock. Just sixty minutes after the time appointed, when the dinner was more of a ruin than a dinner, he arrived in a most amiable mood with Mrs. Whistler, and announced that he never dined before nine. It evidently had never occurred to him that he might have stood a much better chance of getting an unspoiled dinner had he made this grandiloquent statement of his habit in the matter of dining at the time he received the invitation, instead of upon his arrival. He was a past master at making a mint julip. Even Maryland, the home of that delicious drink, I learned later, could not produce a better one.

For all his sharp tongue, I never found Whistler anything but most delightful and amusing. His wit, although caustic and merciless, was so spontaneous, so devoid of spite or bitterness or any ugly depth of feeling, so obviously intended to amuse, that one could not help enjoying it. He himself always seemed perfectly delighted at the setting off of these conversational fireworks. The Whistlers lived in an enchanting pavilion or small house with a very large garden to which one gained access by crossing two immense courtyards. Because of these courtyards and the great garden, the house was so shut away from the turmoil of the city that, once in it one might well imagine oneself to be in the heart of the country.

From Paris—to continue our wedding journey—we went to St. Moritz, in order that I might be presented to Mr. Story's father and mother, who were living in a villa which they had built there. Ours was quite a different journey from that one takes to-day. We went

by rail to Choir, or Chur, and from thence by
diligence to St. Moritz, taking hours for the
drive. The slowness of the locomotion, however, gave us plenty of time to enjoy the magnificent scenery through which, in this day
and age, we are hurled with lightning rapidity.

Upon our arrival at St. Moritz I found my
mother-in-law a woman of heart and understanding and wit. It was a case of love at first
sight with both of us, a love which lasted until
the day of her death in the winter of 1894.

After a delightful visit in St. Moritz, we
drove through the Julia pass down into Italy
to Chiavenna—my first glimpse of that land
of enchantment and beauty—and then on to
Como, where we saw a performance of the then
new opera "Cavalleria Rusticana," in which
Mr. Grau had told me I might possibly sing in
America. From Como we journeyed to Venice, where we were guests at the Palazzo Rez-
zonico, then owned by our friends, the Brownings. "Pen" Browning, it will be remembered,
was the only son of the poets. Pen Browning, christened Robert Barrett Browning, having been born in the Palazzo Guidi in Florence
in the shadow of the Apennines, was called
Pen—Penino—by his father and mother and
intimates.

Venice was a dreamy, poetic place in those days. The only steam driven boat—one which united Venice with the Lido—was followed, on each of its daily trips, by the imprecations of the Venetians, who saw in it the beginning of the desecration of their beloved city. Every one has his motor boat now as well as his gondola, and, though the beauty of the place remains triumphant, and always will, the poetry of life as it was lived then is gone, as is the poetry in most things nowadays.

The days we spent in that lovely old Palazzo, in delightful companionship with the Pen Brownings and their friends, are among my most beautiful and peaceful memories. I devoted an hour or two each day to studying "Cavalleria Rusticana" in the gorgeous monumental ballroom, and then passed the late afternoon and the cool of the evening floating in a gondola through the little canals and lagoons. An occasional evening was spent on the Piazza, where, between crenelations of the surrounding palace walls and the beautiful San Marco campanile, we could see the Italian sky as blue as by day.

We returned to Paris from Venice in order that I might get the necessary clothes and costumes ready for my first American season.

Some Memories and Reflections

This season opened in Chicago in November. Mr. Grau had chosen Chicago for the opening on the theory that if we appeared first in Chicago, that city would receive us without prejudice, whereas, if we played first in New York and were successful, Chicago would instantly adopt a most critical and belligerent attitude toward us. New York, he knew, would form her own opinion regardless and without any danger of being biased.

I had signed with Mr. Grau for this Chicago season and the one to follow in New York, but had refused, upon making the contract in London, to commit myself to a possible supplementary tour of from two weeks to a month that was to include Boston. Mr. Grau, I felt, would give me the same fee for this supplementary tour—and not a very great one it was —if I made good in Chicago and New York, without my signing up for it, and that, should I have a great success, he would give me a larger one if he were unhampered by any previous arrangement; and this is exactly what he did.

Ours was an opera company of stars. All the artists—whose names have already been mentioned—were well established in the operatic world, and had through merit won very high positions. This period, indeed, was known as "the Golden Age of art," for "all-star casts" were drawn up for the theatrical as well as the operatic stage. When in London, Bram Stoker—so many years manager of the Lyceum Theater, and known also as the author of the novel *Dracula*—put at my disposal a box for the famous temple of art, and one of the most memorable performances I saw there was of Shakespeare's "Henry VIII," in which Ellen Terry played the rôle of Catherine of Aragon; Irving, Cardinal Wolsey; Arthur Bouchier, that of Henry VIII, and the incomparable Forbes Robertson took the part of the Duke of Buckingham.

In Grau's "star company," to the astonishment of every one, and to my own more than anybody's, I, who was comparatively a beginner, proved to be the greatest drawing card of the season.

We sang numberless performances of what was then called the "ideal Faust" to a public that was insatiable. The cast of this "ideal Faust" included Jean de Reszke as Faust, Edouard de Reszke as Mephistopheles, Scalchi as Siebel, Lasalles as Valentin, the famous Matilde Baumeister the ubiquitous, as Martha, and myself as Marguerite. In addition to

"Faust," I sang in "Lohengrin" and "Romeo and Juliet"—both with Jean de Reszke—and my only season in "Cavalleria Rusticana."

On this, my first return visit to America, I found New York society perfectly enchanting. There was so much life and gayety in it that one was filled with energy by its very contact, and yet there was just enough of intimacy between its members to make it homelike, an atmosphere that endured only so long as it was protected by what has been called the stiffness and exclusiveness of New York society in the nineties. Those were the days when the Patriarchs' balls (which not a great while later were abandoned because the social climbers who had wormed their way in by hook or by crook at last made them hopelessly promiscuous) flourished in all their glory. The horse show was another of those erstwhile delightful events, where the outsiders, instead of getting into society by usurping the boxes as they had hoped, only pushed society out and changed the entire character of the institution.

Almost all of the old names that were prominent in the latter part of the nineteenth century have disappeared from the columns devoted to social matters in the newspapers. Those that are there now are the names of people of other cities who have since established themselves in New York, and constitute a social group that is possibly as charming and as amusing as the one I knew, but that does not, I am certain, possess the same fine character of simplicity and intimacy.

As I went to America a bride, many dinners were given in my honor in New York. During that first season I went out oftener than I ever did at any future time, as I was too inexperienced to realize I needed to save my strength.

One of the most charming of the many houses where I was entertained was that of those delightful hostesses, Miss Callender and Miss de Forest—lovers of music and the arts, and haters of bores. During my first winter in New York I lived at the St. James's Hotel across Broadway from Delmonico's on 26th Street. These ladies occupied an apartment on Fifth Avenue between 59th and 60th Streets. In a horse-drawn vehicle it was quite a journey to get there. When, however, they moved to a large and beautiful apartment in the Tiffany building in East 72nd Street, one had to allow a full half-hour for the journey. I could devote a long chapter to the changes that have occurred in New York in the intervening years.

MAUDE WETMORE, EMMA EAMES, EMILIO DE GOGORZA,
MISS DE FOREST, AND MISS CALLENDAR

Standing: SIGNORINA SALVINI
Reading from left to right, seated center row: MARCHESE
PERUZZI DE MEDICI, WILLIAM WETMORE STORY, TOM-
MASO SALVINI, EMMA EAMES STORY, MARCHESE
SIMONE PERUZZI DE MEDICI
Seated on ground: BRINDO PERUZZI DE MEDICI, COUNT
CARLO GUICCIARDINI, JULIAN STORY, AND R. B.
BROWNING OR "PEN" (son of the poets, Mr. and Mrs.
R. B. Browning)

SOME MEMORIES AND REFLECTIONS

Miss Callender and Miss de Forest gave the most delightful musical parties in this new apartment, which was perfectly arranged for the purpose. There was an immense music room and a small room on the ground floor, and up a few steps a very large dining room. All their living rooms were on the floor above and were reached by the staircase leading to the dining room, which continued up to a big landing with a balcony, where we sat when we had been dining in intimacy. These were certainly brilliant gatherings, and the most *recherchés* in New York; not only were they *recherchés*, but they were also amusing, the gayety of the occasions being not a little caused by the charm and cordiality of the hostesses, especially of Miss Callender, who had the social gift and a particularly gracious way of dispensing hospitality, receiving her guests with the unconscious and natural air of a person enjoying herself. She sang as an amateur, and although I never heard her sing, the photographs presented to her by such artists as Lili Lehmann, bearing dedications in praise of her talent, are sufficient proof to me of the fact of her gifts.

In 1892 Mrs. Marshall O. Roberts married Colonel Ralph Vivian, and the three colonels

—Colonel Vivian, Colonel Larking and Colonel Stracey—were much sought after in New York society. Mrs. Astor was living in her down-town house on Fifth Avenue, many years before the new one opposite Central Park was built, now in turn destroyed. The first-mentioned house was a miracle of richness and hideousness, but in it she entertained her friends in the real old-fashioned way. Colonel Stracey dining there, was asked by his neighbor if he did not find the dining room beautiful. He deliberately laid down his knife and fork, screwed in his eyeglass, and, carefully examining the room, replied: "If you ask my candid opinion, I think it's d—d ugly!"

In using the term "exclusive," I do not do so in a snobbish way. Certain sets of people, by tradition and environment, end by living together in a circle of a certain intimacy and freedom, almost as one family. Post-war conditions have proved to us that internationalism is an ignorant optimist's dream. Even in one's own country we find some metal that one's melting pot has no effect upon. Certain strata of society, in its larger sense, are units one cannot mix with one another and keep the same in character. I would not presume to say that the character of "smart" society is the only desirable one. I only say that by mixing, it ceases to be what it was and acquires totally different characteristics, to which those of the old school of education and tradition find it difficult to adapt themselves.

The so-called (by Ward McAllister himself, by the way) Four Hundred of New York society, were intensely amused by this snobbish appellation, and as much so by a "character" of that period called Brown, whose business it was to announce the carriages at social functions. It was said that he was heard calling one after another: "Mrs. So-and-So's carriage," and at last: "Mrs. ——'s hired cab stops the way!"

It was during these last years of a fine old century that Maurice Bagby established the nucleus of the now famous and enormously successful Bagby concerts by inviting a few friends to hear some artist of his acquaintance in a little impromptu concert. The audiences of these at first were very small and extremely exclusive, but the idea proved so successful that Mr. Bagby was compelled to move his concerts to the Waldorf Astoria in order to accommodate his guests, and here he charged an entrance fee. Such was his generalship and tact that these musicales never lost their distinction even with their increased popularity. Their success continues through the passing years.

It was in the early nineties, too, that Delmonico's was one of the most delightful places in which to meet one's friends or acquaintances. There were two dining rooms on the main floor, the one on the right of the entrance being the haven of business men who wanted to eat, smoke and talk, undisturbed, and the other on the left, the meeting place of those who were ready to take life less seriously. These were never noisy or overcrowded, and in them one was served delicious food, as delicious as any in France, by servants perfectly trained. Unfortunately, the curious and the "trippers" and the climbers soon transformed this delightful place into a bedlam. To-day, most of the old-time restaurants have been driven out of business by prohibition or jazz or the Charleston. And, as it is with the restaurants, so is it with the concerts and concert halls: quantity and not quality is the rule.

I was always supposed to have gone out a great deal in society. But the contrary was the case after my first season. In the first place, I was not strong enough to endure the excitement of my career and the fireworks it set off inside me, to see all the beautiful things or to do all the reading I wanted to do, to have the long intervals of quiet and solitude so absolutely essential to me in my work, and at the same time to lead a strenuous social life. In the second place, during my whole career I never wasted a moment on the lion hunter. I realized that as long as I was successful such people would flock around me and waste my strength with their parties and petty affairs; but at the same time I knew perfectly well that, should my success wane or I show signs of fatigue, they would be the *first* to say: "Emma Eames is beginning to lose ground." To the public that had been so appreciative and helpful and had the right to the best I could give, I felt I owed all my strength; to the friends who loved me sincerely I owed my love and companionship in as far as my life would allow it; but to the hysteric mob that would follow a celebrated criminal as willingly as a great singer, I felt I had nothing to give. Therefore, I never became a "social butterfly."

On the tour following our New York and Chicago season, the Boston Opera House was unavailable for some reason, and our performances were given at Mechanics Hall in Boston, whose stage was tiny and auditorium mammoth.

Grau had engaged Patti for one performance in Boston. She sang at the matinée—I have forgotten in what opera—preceding the evening performance of our "ideal Faust," and was most annoyed, Mr. Grau told me, to see that in spite of her great name and her great gifts, she had not drawn as big a house as ours. This was due, of course, to the fact that we were the novelty, the new craze, and an unusual stellar combination, while the performance in which she sang depended upon her drawing powers alone. It was unbelievable to me, notwithstanding, after having since my teens worshiped Patti and her greatness as the unattainable, and never dreaming of rivaling her, to find myself playing to a bigger house than hers the very first time I met her on her own ground.

Patti came of the old-style school of singing, in which people learned certain vocal stunts and did them over and over again without variation. Owing to this, and to the fact that she never put any strain upon her voice, never had an atom of bad teaching and had had a perfect vocal placement to begin with, her voice remained a perfect instrument to the end.

The only change was the loss of a few high notes; otherwise her scale retained the same limpid, beautiful quality that had made her famous, until the last day of her career.

The night of our famous "Faust" performance that so annoyed her was one of terrific snow, and yet the crowd, that had had to rely upon a most erratic street-car service for transportation, filled the house to overflowing and was wildly enthusiastic. There were over six thousand people present. As we came out of the stage door after the performance, we found the entire street blocked with people waiting knee-deep in the snow to see us pass. It could not have been a happier return to the city of my early studies and girlhood associations.

I made a most advantageous contract with Mr. Grau for the season of 1892-93 before sailing for Paris, where we stayed a short while and then went to London for the season there.

Thus, at the conclusion of the winter 1891-92, since leaving the Paris Opéra I had been married, had sung my first London season, my first American season, and had paid every cent of my indebtedness.

Incidentally, this same winter also saw me have a bank account that was entirely my own, and draw my first check. Hitherto my mother had never allowed me to have a separate account or to know how much I had. In fact, I had never been given any but the haziest idea of my financial affairs until that winter. When my uncle, General Thomas Hyde, of Civil War fame, decided that I must have my chance in Boston, he and my mother made all the arrangements without taking me into their confidence. And then, after we left Boston and went to Paris, my mother assumed the management and control of all moneys; and it was not until my marriage on August 1, 1891, that I had the handling of the money which I had earned.

During my second London season, in the summer of 1892, I sang a rôle for the first time which I believe came to be much associated with my name in later years, that of the Countess in the "Nozze di Figaro." In addition to the Countess, I created the principal rôle, that of Yasodara, in de Lara's "Light of Asia," with Victor Maurel as Buddha. The "Light of Asia" was de Lara's first essay at writing opera, and proved to be a most touching, melodious and poetic work. Unfortunately, owing to de Lara's inexperience in orchestration, it was not so effective on the stage as it was in a room.

"NOZZE DI FIGARO"
PERIOD LOUIS XIII
1894

SOME MEMORIES AND REFLECTIONS

When the season in London was over we went directly to Italy to join Mr. Story's mother, who was spending the summer in Vallombrosa instead of St. Moritz, because the altitude of the latter had proved too great for her. She was with her daughter, the Marchesa Peruzzi de Medici, whose husband, Simone Peruzzi, completely fulfilled my ideal of the *grand seigneur*. He was a man of great simplicity and feeling, with a very genuine love of the forest and all nature. He was, incidentally, the direct descendant of the family of bankers and exporters that was ruined in the reign of Edward II by the loss in a hurricane of many of its vessels laden with spices and silks and all manner of treasures from the Far East; and by the repudiation on the part of England of the debt to which she had pledged the Crown at the time of the Battle of Crécy, the military preparations for which had been financed by the Peruzzi. Mr. Gladstone, who was a friend of the Storys, tried to do something about the matter, but, although England recognized that the debt incurred at Crécy existed, she said that it would take all the gold in Great Britain, India, and all the colonies to pay it with compound interest.

This family of bankers and importers had

married into the Medici family before the day of the Grand Dukes of Tuscany. My husband's brother-in-law, Simone Peruzzi de Medici, was in no way descended from the great Medicis in the main line. He used to say that the Peruzzi were merchant princes in the Florentine Republic while the Medicis were still rolling pills! The Peruzzi arms may be seen on the façade of the Duomo in Florence with those of the other great families of Tuscany.

The house in which we lived at Vallombrosa was a hunting box belonging to the Medici family (specifically the Great Dukes of Florence) which had become the property of the state, from whom the Peruzzi had leased it for a nominal sum and made it over into a simple, but thoroughly comfortable, summer home. Like all Italian houses of that period, the entrance hall was enormous and filled almost the entire area of the building. It was stone flagged, and was made not only to receive guests, but to house most of the vehicles that were in use. In rainy weather one could drive in, receive passengers and turn round. And there is nothing cramped about a hall in which one can turn a span of horses and a carriage!

As this house belonged to the state, was part

of the property of the domain of Vallombrosa
and could not be bought, the Peruzzi had pur-
chased, not far from it, and surrounded by the
forest of Vallombrosa, a little peasant house
delightfully situated on a piece of free land.
To this they added a number of rooms. That
they were able to find this purchasable bit of
property in the very heart of this state-owned
place was due to a peculiar law about land in
Italy, which we were to encounter later when
we came to buy the ground on which we built.
This law permits one to buy a large area of
land as such, but within that area dozens of
peasants may still own plots and retain title
and dispose of their property to you separately,
if they wish, after the principal transaction is
completed.

Mr. Story's sister, the Marchesa, had three
children, two of whom were at those extremely
interesting and amusing ages of eleven and
fourteen, respectively. With them we roamed
the forest of Vallombrosa in fustian clothes
the whole day long. And in the evening they
would act the most amusing charades for us,
displaying a genuine gift for comedy and not
a little histrionic ability.

At the end of this happy summer with my
husband's family and just as Julian and I were

preparing to return to Paris and I was beginning to look forward eagerly to my next season, we heard that the Metropolitan Opera House had been gutted by fire, and that there would be no American season!

IV

SHORTLY after I heard of the burning of the Metropolitan I was taken ill, and the autumn of 1892 was spent under the care of a physician. I have never had any desire to excite compassion in the hearts of either my friends or my public. One who is pitied is never fully believed in or admired. But during my entire career I never knew a day without pain, and my private life was not a happy one. Yet I believe I can congratulate myself on having impressed all who knew me as always being perfectly well and perfectly happy.

Between my illness, the canceled American season, the knowledge that all the money I had earned had gone to pay my debts, and my anxiety as to when I could or would sing again, that autumn of 1892 managed to be a most depressing one—so much so, that when I received an offer, at the end of November, to go to Spain to sing Elsa in "Lohengrin" in December, I accepted immediately, and got up from my bed in order to fill the engagement, a rash proceeding for which I was to pay in full later.

This month's engagement in Spain, in spite of the effort it entailed, proved to have many compensations. One of them was that a most charming woman, Madame de Osma, whom I had met at Mrs. Post's in Paris, and with whom I had formed a friendship, was in Spain at the time and introduced Julian and me to some of the most delightful people in Madrid, including the Duchesse de Sesto, the Duques de Santonia, the Marquesa Manzanedo, the Duc and Duchesse d'Albe, and Sir Henry Drummond Woolfe, the British Ambassador, and we were widely entertained.

Madame de Osma was the daughter of the Conde de Valencia, and the Count, interestingly enough, was not her father, but her *mother,* a paradox brought about by the Salic law in Spain, which permits the women of a family to inherit title failing a male heir. Her father's name was Crook. He was the same who was responsible for the wonderful collection of swords and armor and other accouterments of war on exhibition at the Armería in Madrid. This collection contains an equestrian statue in wood of Charles V, wearing his authentic costume of the period and in full armor, the horse also being in complete war panoply. It also comprises the sedan chair in which Philip II used to travel from Madrid to the Escurial, and the beautiful tent of Francis I, which was captured at the Battle of Pavia. Our Spanish hosts gave several unique parties for us. After my first performance in "Lohengrin," the artist Madrazo arranged a musical evening at his studio at which several gypsy women who had heard me the night before as Elsa, demonstrated in turn for me their art of singing. During the course of the afternoon one of these gypsy singers offered me a glass of wine, which I was about to refuse when I caught my host surreptitiously signaling me to drink it. He afterwards explained that had I not done so the singers would have been gravely affronted, would have considered that I wished to indicate that I despised them, and would probably have left the house at once.

On the informal program with these gypsies was a beautiful, tall, slender young woman from Seville, who danced for us. She was lovely, and the impression she made that day was only equaled in later years by the famous Pastora Imperio.

Another unusual musical party was one given by the Marquesa Manzanedo, who en-

gaged a very old and very celebrated *guitarrista*
to come to her house one evening to sing and
play for me. This playing and singing consisted of a long quivering brushing of the
strings in Oriental modulations, and at intervals, to the unaccustomed ear without reason,
sudden ejaculations on the part of the singer
almost spoken rather than sung, with equally
abrupt silences. In spite of my ignorance of
the Spanish language and my bewilderment at
this kind of music, I was most strangely
thrilled by it.

Another who made our visit to Spain delightful was that interesting and intellectual
woman, the Duchesse d'Albe, to whom we
owe the discovery of a great number of the
original documents of Cervantes and Columbus. The circumstances that led to her finding
these invaluable parchments were rather interesting and not without a feminine angle. After
her marriage to the Duc d'Albe she became
exceedingly curious about the contents of the
various storerooms in the palace at Madrid,
and one day started on a tour of investigation.
This tour brought to light many boxes filled
with old documents, and these documents
proved to be the great treasures of Cervantes
and Columbus. Those who attended the

World's Fair in Chicago in 1893 may recall seeing some of them, as the Duchesse sent a number to be placed on exhibition there.

Her husband, the Duc d'Albe, was a great lover of sport, but was so exceedingly small—although extremely well made—that he had to be strapped on the box of his coach and have bands of leather fastened about his wrists, in order to be able to drive his four-in-hand. And yet this miniature of a man proved to us beyond the shadow of a doubt that he was larger than his ancestor, the famous Duke of the Wars of the Netherlands, whose heroic deeds would have seemed to be possible only to a physical colossus. But such was not the case, for when our Duc d'Albe wanted to wear his mighty ancestor's armor to a fancy-dress ball, he found it was so much too small for him that he could not get into it! Apparently size has nothing to do with valor.

It was Sir Henry Drummond Woolfe, however, who, in making our Christmas a real English Christmas, put the crowning touch to our delightful sojourn in Spain.

After that I had a relapse as payment for my good times, and had to be hurried back to Paris and to bed, where I remained until a short time before I left for London and the season there.

It was during that season—in 1893—that I sang my first performance of the "Nozze di Figaro" in London. I took the rôle of the Countess; Madame Nordica that of Susanna; Zélie de Lussan, Cherubino; Edouard de Reszke, the Count; and Maurel, Figaro. Because Edouard de Reszke was believed to be too large to look well in the costumes of the Louis XV period, we were told that we must wear those of the Louis XIII—or Henrietta Maria period, as it was called in England—and forthwith I had some made in London from my own designs.

That was the year that I created the rôle of the heroine in L. E. Bach's "Lady of Longford," and it was through this rôle that I came to know the real Lady of Longford, now the Dowager Countess of Radnor. Before her husband had succeeded to his father's title, the real Lady of Longford, then known as Lady Folkstone, had acquired a considerable reputation as a beautiful and successful amateur singer. And after she became the Countess of Radnor she organized an orchestra of ladies and led it herself for many years, devoting much time to the work. It was during this period that I came to know her well. Bach's opera, "The Lady of Longford," did not survive, but at least it was the means of my making a most delightful and enduring friendship. Eva, in "The Meistersinger," was another new rôle that I added to my repertoire that season. I sang it in Italian with Jean de Reszke, Edouard de Reszke and the great Pol Plançon. This translation was made by a rather unprosperous Italian named Mezzucato. Signor Mezzucato deserved a far greater place in the world of literature than the one conceded to him, for his translation was masterly. It adhered strictly to the meaning of the original text, and at the same time had a decent regard for the value of the notes and the rhythm. I believe it was never published. We learned it, at least, from a score in which it had been interpolated in red ink in his own handwriting.

It was that season in London that I sang Elizabeth in French, apropos of which one of the administrators of the opera made the astounding statement that Wagner would soon never be heard in any language but French.

That year I sang again by command at a Buckingham Palace concert, an event that is really worth a paragraph or two of description. The Buckingham Palace concerts took place in the great ballroom of the Palace. At one end was the stage, and at the other, the daïs upon which were placed the thrones of the Prince and Princess of Wales, who always represented the Queen on these occasions, and the court. On either side of the great room were tiers of seats for the audience, which faced neither the thrones nor the stage, but a broad aisle, perhaps thirty feet wide, which extended the length of the vast room. As it was an occasion that called for every one's most magnificent attire, jewels, uniforms and decorations—those not in uniform wore knee breeches and all the orders they might possess, including the Order of the Garter with its beautiful blue ribbon. The audience, when seated in all its sartorial splendor, made each side of the room look like an opened jewel casket filled to overflowing.

One of the least charming features of singing at these concerts was the fact that one must take one's place on the stage before the arrival of royalty, and remain there until the end of the concert. When the guests were in their places and the singers on the stage, the royal procession entered through the door at the right of the stage. It was headed by the Lord Chamberlain—the White Stick—carrying a slender, peeled willow wand and walking backwards so that he would always face royalty. Imagine the practice it must have taken him to walk backwards the entire length of that enormous room with so much grace and dignity.

There was no applause after we sang, as etiquette forbade it, but the dear Prince had so much courtesy of the heart that he could never resist making the *gesture* of applause.

One of the court chamberlains of that period, of whom I saw a great deal during those early years of my career in London, and, in fact, every year until his death, was a delightful and handsome man called Lord Lathom, who was subsequently given an earldom by Queen Victoria. Lord Lathom had a unique distinction and one for which he was celebrated. He had a beautiful curly white beard, and in spite of the smuts of London it was never anything but immaculate.

At the conclusion of this season in London it was considered inadvisable for me to take the trip to Italy. Therefore, Julian went to Vallombrosa alone to see his mother, while I remained in Paris to prepare for the coming season at the Metropolitan, that of 1893-94.

Of the many problems that confronted me during my career, not the least was to find some way to get through the day that I was to sing to the best advantage. I tried everything, experimented with every kind of diet and relaxation, and at last adopted the suggestion of Zélie de Lussan, of having one meal in the day always at the same hour—one o'clock —and on the days I sang suppressing the evening meal altogether; and also, in so far as I could, avoiding all thought of the imminent performance. After my one o'clock meal I sat about quietly for an hour and then took a two-hours' rest. I had acquired such control of mind and nerves that I could instantly lapse into a state of complete unconsciousness which endured the whole of those two hours. At its conclusion I was quietly awakened, and just before it was time for me to go to the theater I was given a cup of tea, and that was my last mouthful until after the opera was over.

I departed from this practice only twice. The first time was when I attended a luncheon given by one of the great London hostesses, the Marquesa Santurce, at the resquest of the Duke of Connaught, who had expressed a desire to meet me, on the very day that, owing to an unexpected change of bill I was to sing Marguerite in "Faust" at Covent Garden.

Needless to say, I did both, and was none the worse.

The second time was during the season in New York of which I am about to speak, that of 1893-94, when Madame Nordica gave a big luncheon at Delmonico's on the day that I was to sing Micaela in "Carmen" in Brooklyn.

Another of my operatic problems was to overcome my consciousness of my audience. Being terribly sensitive, the mere thought of being observed by all those eyes troubled me to such an extent that I had great difficulty in concentrating upon the work in hand. The struggle became so great that at last I was obliged to imagine that the stage had four walls and that the music drama was an actuality and not a "counterfeit presentment," in order to do myself justice, unhindered by the consciousness of being observed.

About six weeks before the next American season, I discovered that I was making too much effort for too little vocal result, was using unnecessary muscles and had certain difficulties of vocal emission; and, as I did not wish to wait until the public had found it out, too, I began to look about me for a means by which I might correct these faults. I found this means in Paris by a most lucky chance, in the person of that great voice tuner, Madame de Picciotto, who is not to be confounded with her daughter-in-law, the pianist, who later became a vocal teacher.

This old lady had the finest ear imaginable, and seemed able to catch the slightest deviation from the perfect vocal line. The moment I talked with her I knew that I had come to the right person, and I put myself immediately into her hands, although, as I have said, it was only six weeks before my next American season.

She told me that I used unnecessary effort in singing my middle notes, an effort which shortened my voice at both ends. She taught me to overcome this and gain security of vocal emission by concentrating on the vibratory sensation of the voice in the throat and head instead of listening to the sound of my voice. Although I was unable at first to hear two or three notes in my voice by this method, I had such faith in her that I obeyed her implicitly.

At the end of two weeks I found I had endless breath in singing and my tone had a warmth of quality that it had never possessed before. With the succeeding weeks my voice grew in security, ease and depth, and when I left Madame de Picciotto, it was capable of effects of color and accent hitherto dangerous or impossible, and of undertaking the heavier rôles which I was to add later to my repertoire. Furthermore, this simplifying of my vocal method enabled me at last to forget my voice and devote myself to my interpretations. My great desire had always been to create the complete illusion: to make my audience forget me and think only of the character I was portraying. To do this I went down into my soul for that part of it that might have belonged to the character to be represented, and that bit of my entity I dedicated from that time forth to that particular rôle. This is the reason, too, why I was never able to experiment with my interpretations. As I first conceived them, so they remained, at least basically, until the end.

I was told that I was considered cold in such rôles as Elsa in "Lohengrin," but, as I have pointed out, it would have been impossible for me to modify my interpretation even had I so desired, for I had conceived Elsa as a medieval princess, sheltered, mentally undeveloped—as any student of history knows the young girls of that period were—gentle, dreamy, impressionable, poetic, overwhelmed with grief at the loss of her brother and an easy prey for the bullying militant Ortrud. Such negativeness was the only possible excuse for the lack of loyalty and honor she displayed when she asked Lohengrin the forbidden question. Then, too, there must be a contrast between her character and that of Ortrud. If Elsa and Ortrud are equally passionate and explosive, the scene before the church in the second act degenerates into nothing more or less than a fishwives' quarrel. I always gave this scene a note of shocked surprise and indignation, and I am very glad to say that there were many in my audiences at that time who understood and appreciated my interpretation of Elsa.

Another rôle of mine about which the realists were inclined to quarrel was that of Marguerite in Gounod's "Faust." Gounod's Marguerite was not the bold peasant of Goethe's great poem, but a figure of his own, consistent with those of Kaulbach's illustration, upon which the traditional costumes of the Marguerite of that period were based.

The story is a sordid one unless idealized, and I preferred to see Marguerite as chaste, truly innocent and therefore unsuspecting, and that is why I made her fearlessly and directly look at Faust when he accosted her, aware of no evil, but wrapped in poetic dreams. The

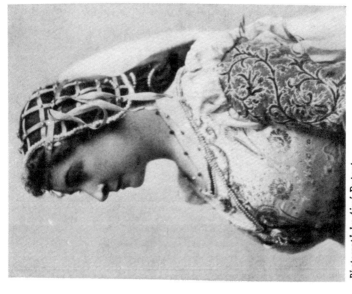

As Desdemona in "Otello"

As Elsa in "Lohengrin"

school of realism destroys all the meaning of such operas; and often the realistic actress is not a reflecting or intelligent artist, but one who prefers to portray her own unbridled self and blow off steam, rather than sink her personality in that of the character she is portraying.

Jean de Reszke, with whom I sang Marguerite and Elsa, as well as Juliette, was, fortunately for me, a true poet and a romantic, and our interpretations did not jar on each other. Another great artist among the men to whom I must give my homage was Pol Plançon. Plançon was a singer of elegance, taste, grace and perfection of diction, as well as a great actor. And the evenings when both he and Jean were in the cast were, with me, little short of heaven. I was always a little in love with Jean, anyway, when we were singing together.

There was a fable that went the rounds during those years I sang with Jean to the effect that Julian was terrifically jealous of him. People used to watch Julian at my performances, and fancied they discovered many evidences of his feeling in the matter. The truth was that Julian, passionately interested in my career, and keenly aware of my nervousness over each public appearance, clenched his

147

hands from anxiety and not from jealousy.

To be a successful opera singer one must have both the instinct for singing and the instinct for the theatrical. As I have said, I inclined more toward the dramatic than the vocal, and my histrionic gift made me seek to convince my audience with very few, but significant, gestures. I always felt that it was better to stand perfectly still than to make any movement that might blur the meaning. The windmill variety of acting never appealed to me, and I found that, although the public, reacting to sheer magnetism, will often rise to the elemental and the melodramatic, even though meretricious, it will also always respond to the fine and sincere.

Experience was my teacher: finish and versatility are not born of youth. These fruits of a many-faceted imagination which enable one to do the thing not native to one's nature, come only with artistic maturity. I was always an ardent advocate of that method of study that made those great Italian actors, Ristori, Salvini and Rossi, celebrated. In their day when an actor evinced a decided talent for tragedy he was obliged first to become a convincing comedian; if he showed a flair for comedy, he was made to study until he could bring tears

148

of horror in tragedy. That was not the time, as now, when a rôle was fitted to an artist as if it were a dress. Oh, this modern type system that demands only a few tricks, a personality and self-confidence! There was nothing of it in that early Italian method. In that, one had to be master of one's technic.

My career imposed many restrictions upon me. For instance, I never dared read a newspaper. Having an emotional nature that was ready to respond to and dramatize any suggestion, I became horribly agitated upon reading of murders, suicides, robberies and sordid political juggling, and had to abandon my daily paper altogether. The result was that I often did not know when my acquaintances died or were married. Then, during an opera or concert season, upon the evening preceding the performance I could never go to parties, and I never dared to lunch or dine out or go to the theater, even informally with close friends.

In the latter years I sang less frequently, but my health was such then that I had only strength for my work. As I averaged ten performances a month during the early part of my career, and as my opera seasons in America and London absorbed the greater part of the year, it can readily be seen that my work possessed me body and soul. Fortunately, it gave me the joy of which Stevenson speaks, the "work that is play."

During the season of 1893-94 I added, as I have said, Micaela in "Carmen" to my repertoire, in order that I might help Maurice Grau to produce it with his complete all-star cast, at raised prices. This cast was composed of Calvé as Carmen, probably the greatest Carmen that ever has been or ever will be; Jean de Reszke as Don José, myself as Micaela and Plançon as Escamillio. The latter sang the famous toreador rôle in a beard—perish the thought—but sang it so incomparably that he could have worn anything and been forgiven.

Other rôles I sang that season were Mistress Ford in the "Merry Wives of Windsor," with Victor Maurel as Falstaff and a cast which included Zélie de Lussan; Dona Elvira in "Don Giovanni," with Nordica as Dona Anna and Zélie de Lussan as Zerlina. In this last opera Nordica and de Lussan and myself supported Victor Maurel in his famous rôle of Don Juan, and he was so anxious for us to be willing to sing these rather boring rôles as often as he wished, that he sent each of us immense bouquets of violets the night of the performance to keep us in a good temper. None of the above rôles were calculated to add to the glory of a prima donna, but I was intensely interested in doing them. And as it was always my conviction that it is not what one sings so much as the way one sings it that counts, I felt that I did not demean myself by appearing in rôles not strictly considered as those of a prima donna.

Incidentally, Victor Maurel was indirectly responsible for the coining of a name for music critics that afterwards became quite famous. In those years music criticism in America was exceedingly primitive. One day, when a friend who was with me on tour that season, read a criticism of Maurel just a little more idiotic than the general run, she made a point of establishing the identity of this particular "critic." At last she discovered that he was employed during the day as an opener of oysters in a certain oyster bar in that town, and wrote music criticism at night. From that day to this she has never designated the dignified group of men who sit in judgment on the musical world as anything but "oyster openers."

Tamagno was with us that season, and he and Victor Maurel and I sang in many performances of "Otello" together, taking the rôles of Otello, Iago and Desdemona respectively. Tamagno was the perfect Otello. No one could have been more convincing in the rôle. Certain of my friends used to say they feared for my life during the performances that I sang with him, because he always flung me about with such violence. He must have had something of the same fear, for after he had thrown me on the bed preparatory to smothering me, he always would murmur contritely that he hoped he hadn't hurt me.

Once when singing "Otello" in Monte Carlo with him, on a very small stage and with most inadequate scenery and props, he flung me down with such violence that the back legs of the bed, which were only nailed to the rear of the platform, collapsed; and it was only by clinging to the bed with all my strength that I kept myself from rolling down behind it. It may give some idea of the fervor with which the scene was acted to tell that not one person in the audience laughed.

This same season saw the first performance in America of Massenet's "Werther." Jean de Reszke took the name part, and I sang Charlotte. Charlotte was a rather strange rôle for a soprano to undertake, as all its effects were in the medium and low voice, but fortunately my voice, in addition to the soprano, had the notes and quality of the mezzo and contralto, and managed an A below the staff quite as easily as any other note in its range.

On the tour that year, which for some reason preceded our season in New York, I was the victim of a most painful accident that was quite my own doing. We left St. Louis on a special train that was to take us to Boston and, upon finding that the door of the drawing-room which I occupied refused to remain closed, I got up and slammed it too hastily to note that my fingers were caught in the jamb. As a result, the nail of my forefinger was torn out by the roots and the nail of the third finger terribly crushed. The friend who was traveling with me sent for the conductor at once, and begged him to get a doctor at the nearest station. In the meantime I plunged my mangled fingers into an antiseptic extract, then settled myself in bed with my hand up so that the blood should run away from my fingers, and waited for the doctor—several hours, alas! Finally the train was stopped at a tiny town whose name I do not recall, and a doctor was summoned. Unfortunately, he was so thrilled at being called to attend a prima donna that he could do nothing for me whatsoever—unless one could call the two or three little morphine pellets he gave me to take when the pain became unbearable, adequate aid!

This was on Monday. Upon our arrival in Boston on Tuesday I sent for that great surgeon, Dr. Porter, and was told by him that there was nothing to do but extract both nails. As I was advertised to sing in the "Nozze di Figaro" on Wednesday, I told him that my hand would have to wait, as I would not disappoint my audience; and he finally permitted me to sing the Countess with my arm in a sling, and, incidentally, as well as I ever did in my life. The next morning the operation was performed. Two days after this painful experience, on Saturday, I sang Marguerite at the matinée. This was the first of the two times that season that I was to sing in "Faust" immediately after an operation. The second was four days after an overenthusiastic physician who had caught the current craze for nose operations, had carved a small piece of bone out of my nose—although there was no real need for such an operation—and had allowed me to walk home afterwards through the snow with a hemorrhage!

I had been persuaded by Jean de Reszke to consult this physician for general advice, although I had no definite reason for doing so.

SOME MEMORIES AND REFLECTIONS

Jean de Reszke was one of the most apprehensive singers imaginable, and wore an expression of terror in his eyes during the whole performance. He always had with him a laryngoscope and frequently examined his throat and larynx. This winter he had found a congenial spirit in this really very great throat specialist and surgeon. Before this time—1893-94— no one had thought of consulting a throat specialist unless actually ill or diseased. Jean made it the fashion for singers to be treated, and persuaded me to be examined, although there was nothing the matter with me, with the above result. There was another result that was even more harmful. In those days the properties, drawbacks and reactions of cocaine were not fully realized. This doctor actually gave us weak solutions of cocaine to use in our noses with an atomizer, saying it made the voice more brilliant. I soon learned that it also relaxed it so terrifically on the rebound that its use was suicidal. Jean de Reszke always went to this doctor before a performance, and almost invariably smelled of iodoform and ether through the whole of the opera. To be thinking of the throat and the mechanism of tone production is simply paralyzing and devastating. That small fraction of one's body is only a very tiny part of the singing apparatus, and many people sing even better in spite of physical disabilities—if unconscious of them—if the moral and mental conditions are propitious. To be boosted into singing by local treatments of any kind is a criminal mistake. Before the above fad—happily in the case of the more enlightened practitioners nearly past —singers never imagined rushing to a throat specialist if hoarse or otherwise vocally under a cloud, but had recourse to ordinary hygienic means and, above all, rest and quiet.

During this season there was an epidemic of influenza which laid us all low in turn. In Philadelphia I sang Marguerite in "Faust" with a temperature of 104 F., and again in Brooklyn, with this same kind but overenthusiastic doctor in the wings ready to administer digitalis if my heart gave out, as it threatened to do. He was obsessed with the idea of making us sing under all conditions, a very mistaken idea as far as we were concerned, but as I said before, he was a great surgeon. After this season, I reverted to the methods of the old school and counted on nature and rest for healing without resorting to treatment.

It would not be amiss, perhaps, while chronicling these first years of my success in the famous rôle of the Countess in the "Nozze di Figaro," to mention the costumes that were made for me for that opera by Jean Philippe Worth.

When I had first gone to the great Worth establishment I had asked, naturally, to see the original Worth, the famous couturier to the Empress Eugénie and her court, and he had turned me over to his son, Jean Philippe. I found Jean Philippe to be the type that could have been a great artist in any métier he might have chosen. He had a perfect sense of balance, color and line. Prior to the Countess costumes, he had only made one simple but very beautiful evening dress for me: but in the "Nozze di Figaro" his art had full play, and the result was epoch-making. When I first appeared in his costumes it was said that I looked as though I had just stepped out of a Van Dyck painting.

He also designed my Marguerite costumes. Before we decided upon the style of the latter we made a profound study of a book containing reproductions of Albrecht Dürer's engravings—a very nearly complete collection—and chose the ones we considered best suited to me. Sargent rewarded this labor by declaring Worth's Marguerite costumes to be the only perfect ones he had ever seen worn by Gounod's heroine. And incidentally, M. Worth never ceased to declare himself grateful to me for my having permitted him to dress Marguerite, in the church scene, in black and white instead of the usual violet cashmere robe of tradition.

As I considered my wigs of quite as much importance as my costumes, I had them made for me specially by Auguste Petit, who used only the finest quality of naturally curly hair in their construction, and "planted" it, as the wigmaker's phrase goes, exactly as my own hair grew. Indeed, they were made with such care and exactitude that they could have been worn very well in real life as well as on the stage.

In the beginning I had used my own hair, particularly in such rôles as Juliette and Marguerite. I had done this with the idea of keeping my head small, as nothing adds so much to the elegance of appearance or to the illusion of height as a small head. As all artists know, the eye unconsciously measures the height of a man by the size of his head—he is six heads high, or seven or eight heads high, as the case may be. And I desired to appear tall.

My own hair was dark, but I had many

Photograph by Aimé Dupont

IN "BALLO IN MASCHERA"

precedents for wearing dark hair as Marguerite and, of course, as Juliette. There was much discussion at the time, I remember, over my not wearing a blond wig in Elsa, a discussion that annoyed me extremely and betrayed me into making one or two sharp remarks. I believe one of them was that if a blond wig were absolutely necessary to the enjoyment of the audience, I would have one put on a pole on the stage, but that I would not wear it.

However, I came to wigs in time, because certain rôles demanded them. In the "Ballo in Maschera" I wore a *blond-cendré* wig. The hair of Rubens' wife, Helena Fourment, in the portrait of her painted by her husband, is the same lovely blond-ash-colored tint. In Pamina my wig was flaxen; in Sieglinde, the veritable haystack of tradition which, although I restrained it within the lines of beauty, was as fabulous as Wagner's stories. In the "Nozze di Figaro" of 1907—where I wore the costumes of the Louis XV period, which replaced those destroyed in the San Francisco earthquake—my wig was tiny and ash blond. In the gala scene I wore it slightly powdered.

Following the season of 1893-94 in America I again sang in London, appearing in the new rôles which that strenuous year at the Metropolitan had added to my repertoire. It was in this London season that I had the pleasure of singing with Sembrich in the "Nozze di Figaro" for the first of the myriad times we were to appear in that opera together. I had heard Sembrich first in 1884 or 1885 in Boston, and she had seemed, as had Patti, another of those bright, beautiful stars beyond the range of any ambition of mine. Her voice was of the purest, most crystalline and limpid quality, and possessed of that musical distinction which was typical of her entire career. Incidentally, this London début of hers was a most unfair one for her. She had been engaged for the season with the distinct understanding that she was to make her bow in the rôle of Violetta in "Traviata." But for some reason, she was not allowed to do so, and instead was obliged to make her début as Susanna in the "Nozze," which gave her very little scope, and in which her great aria occurs only in the last act. She was and still is a very great artist and a most charming woman.

This changing of the opera billed at the last moment amounted, in London, almost to a vice. During this season I was to sing in a command performance of "Romeo and Juliet" before Queen Victoria at Windsor Castle, but

Jean de Reszke fell strangely ill, and "Carmen" was substituted. This particular substitution, it is perhaps significant to note, compelled me to make my operatic bow before the Queen in a secondary rôle, that of Micaela.

The preceding autumn we had given orders for the enlargement of our house in the Place des États-Unis, and after the London season had run its course we went to Paris to become acquainted with and settled in our new house. I was extremely tired when it was all done. The American and London seasons had been strenuous enough without the additional strain of putting a new home in order; nevertheless, I found the strength somewhere to go to Italy with Julian. His dear mother had died that winter, and he wanted me to go with him to see his father.

Those wonderful Vallombrosa woods! Like Antæus, I always gained strength from contact with my mother earth. This beautiful summer in Vallombrosa was just what I needed to prepare me for the following winter's work in America.

While in Italy that summer I made the acquaintance of the great actor Tommaso Salvini, whose son, Alessandro, had a brief but brilliant career in America. I had seen Tommaso Salvini act in my student days in Boston. He played the rôle of Othello in Italian, while the rest of the company, including Edwin Booth as Iago, and Marie Wainwright as Ophelia, acted in English. I felt I ought to admire Salvini, but I did not thrill to an obese and rather bombastic person, as it seemed to my inexperienced ear, so badly dressed and entirely out of tune in his Italian conception with that of the Anglo-Saxons with whom he was acting. I little thought I was going to take part in performances equally ludicrous, singing two acts of one opera in Italian and one in French in "Faust" and in "Carmen," owing to the illness of both Calvé and Jean de Reszke, singing myself in French, the tenor, de Lucia, in Italian, while the Carmen, Basta Tavari, sang in German.

Salvini came often to the Peruzzi's villa from Vallombrosa-Saltino, where he and his daughter were passing the summer at one of its very primitive hotels of that time. My nephew, Bindo Peruzzi, told the story that lunching one day with Salvini at his hotel the usual athletic Italian country chickens were served, with the result of the squeaking and scratching of knives in the effort at dissection. At each of these sounds Salvini would wince and draw

SOME MEMORIES AND REFLECTIONS

his breath noisily. At last, able to bear it no longer, he rose, cast a devastating glance over the dining room, and exclaiming in stentorian accents: *"Quando avrete finito tornero in questa segheria"* (When you have finished, I will return to this sawmill), walked majestically out.

Many and long-winded were the arguments between W. W. Story (my father-in-law) and Salvini apropos of the interpretations of Shakespeare, to which we listened respectfully. Salvini had a most charming and amiable manner, and one of my lost but cherished possessions was a note written by him to me for my birthday the following summer, when I was unable to leave Paris.

That winter, the one of 1894-95, was marred by only one ugly and outrageous incident. One of the editors or directors of a certain musical paper, after failing to get in touch with me directly, sent me a very carefully written letter in which he informed me that I might have the good will of his paper for five thousand dollars a year! Greatly indignant at this thinly disguised attempt at intimidation and knowing that most interesting of attorneys, Joseph H. Choate, very well at the time, I immediately took the letter to him. I also told him of similar overtures made to various other artists of the company, including Van Dyke. Mr. Choate took charge of the letter, and dealt with its author so vigorously that not only was I never bothered again, but the paper never dared attack me as it ordinarily would have done upon my refusal to pay tribute.

Many years afterwards, when I made a concert tour under the direction of the Wolfsohn Bureau, Mr. Wolfsohn asked me what I wished to do about advertising in the musical papers. I told him that I not only refused to have anything to do with them, but that I forbade him to do anything himself in my behalf. When he wanted to know my reason for this attitude, I said that such advertising was of no practical value, as the only people who read those papers anyway were the deadheads.

This season that I took my stand against the musical papers in America, and the one that followed it in London, I merely repeated the operas that were already in my repertoire. In the autumn of that year I was again laid low by illness, an indisposition preceded by a terrible chill that had come upon me as I was returning from Rome, where I had gone with my husband to attend his father's funeral.

In spite of this illness, however, the winter

of 1895-96 in Paris was very far from being dismal. We knew the charming Lord and Lady Dufferin intimately, as well as many members of the British Embassy; and as I was not so ill that I could not see my friends, a number of very delightful parties helped me through the tedium of an idle season. I recovered my health in time to fulfil my engagement at Covent Garden in the spring. We spent many week-ends—as indeed we did every year in London—at the enchanting home of Howard Sturgis, the writer, whom I have mentioned before. Among other things, Howard had a most amusing collection of dogs: a St. Bernard called Baloo; a collie, Nancy; a Welsh terrier lengthily named Tess of the d'Urbervilles, and a fox terrier answering to Rags. In addition to these four, there was a strange little animal of excellent breed that looked like a pom, belonging to one of the other guests, and my beloved Peeny.

Peeny was the most interesting and charming person imaginable—to me she was never merely a dachshund—and was welcomed upon her arrival with me each year in America, with headlines in all the papers. These six animals, representing many breeds and sizes and dispositions, a perfect League of Nations of dogdom, played together the whole day long in perfect amity. One great game they had was running a kind of race in a circle. My little dog, having no speed whatsoever on account of her short dachshund legs, nevertheless was always certain that she had won, because the others after running circles around her, sooner or later finished up behind her. And when this point came, she invariably left the circle with an air of great triumph.

Mr. Story owned two dachshunds when we were married and, as I had never been permitted to have a pet when I was a little girl, although I had always dreamed of owning one, these were my first canine friends. I must admit, however, that when I first saw a dachshund I thought it the most monstrous and dismal of animals; but after I really got acquainted with dogs of this breed, I came to know them for the amusing creatures they are. However, one never has but one perfect companion in dogdom, no matter how many one may own—and we had many at various times —and my dear Peeny, who was so vain about her success as a Marathon runner, was that companion to me.

On one of these visits to Windsor and Howard Sturgis, I sang for the Eton boys one after-

166

IN PRIVATE LIFE WITH "PEENY"
1897

noon in St. George's Chapel. Sir Walter Parratt, the court organist, was my accompanist. It was a most interesting experience. From my vantage point in the organ loft I could look down on the chapel filled with eager, young upturned faces. We had tried to keep the affair a secret from the royal family, the members of which were all very fond of music in those days; but the Princess Pat—now Lady Patricia Ramsay—and the Princess Christian, came in quietly to listen unobserved—so they thought!—in a distant corner.

Another joy of my sojourns in London was the zoölogical gardens, where I ended by knowing every keeper and caressing every animal that was approachable, no matter of what species. Incidentally, the Chicago Zoo was another animal refuge where I was equally well known. I remember assisting at the christening of some lion cubs that were born during one of the Chicago seasons, holding the little one who was to be named "Emma Eames" in my arms. I regret to state that this particular animal grew up to be so violent and so fierce that, after seriously wounding most of her keepers, she had to be put to death.

The season of 1896-97 saw me again at the Metropolitan, but so far as I can remember,

I added no new rôles to my repertoire that year.

This winter which, professionally, had been a most brilliant one for me, is nevertheless shrouded in my memory by a terrible emotion in my private life, for in it I had a great hope and a great disappointment. In February it was decided that I must undergo a most serious operation, and one to which I should never have submitted had I been told the risk and the probable outcome. In as much as my life was in danger whether the operation was performed or not, I should have preferred to let nature take her course. However, others took the matter into their hands, and . . . perhaps, after all, it was fate.

It was during this terrible time that Miss Fanny Fetridge, my inseparable companion through all the latter part of my career, began her many years of loving care of me. This dearest of friends having recently lost her father, was in the deepest mourning. She was a much beloved and sought after member of society in Paris. My dear friends, Miss Callender and Miss de Forest, who were devoted to her, invited her to pass the winter with them in New York, and go with them to the opera and the theater, of which they were most assiduous frequenters. This friend of my heart, therefore, was on the spot when I needed her most, as she always was afterwards, both in my personal and public life. Her warm heart immediately prompted her to leave her other friends and the luxurious surroundings to take care of me and stand between me and all annoyances. While I was ill she read aloud to me in the most simple and perfect manner, making all she read real. I remember that, when I was alive enough to listen, she read to me Barrie's *Sentimental Tommy,* a joy and a delight; but of which I could only have infinitesimal doses at first, as I was so convulsed with amusement by it, and laughing to that extent was painful. Dear, patient Fanny! As I dictated the first lines about her I learned of her death in England after a very short illness to which such a climax had not been expected— and I was not with her! Darling Fanny, so human, so loving, so amusing and tactful, so unobtrusive and gentle—such a wonderful genius for friendship! She has gone, and in going she has taken a great part of my life with her.

I did not fully realize it at the time, but I never could have carried on the last twelve years of my career except for her tender solicitude. During those years she stood between me and all the importunities that are the penalty of the operatic life. She explained any inevitable negligence on my part to my friends, who were her friends as well, and arranged for me to see them when I could. She kept all the little worries from me, and smoothed away all unpleasantness with a tact and graciousness that would have made her a splendid wife of a diplomat. How much, also, do I owe to her wise advice!

As time went on it became more and more difficult for me to endure any added fatigue or strain outside that entailed by my work. It is said that one's body and nerves remember every shock and illness, and that their power of resistance and recovery is lessened by each new onslaught. I am certain that this was so in my own case.

Exactly three months after that operation in February—a much greater shock to my nerves than it would have been in this day of advanced surgery and anæsthetics—I was singing in London. It was the Jubilee year, and not to be missed if it were humanly possible for me to profit by it. A detail of my participation in this memorable celebration of the fiftieth year of Queen Victoria's reign was the presentation to me by the Prince of Wales of two seats in his stand at Buckingham Palace from which we might view the Jubilee Procession. I accepted them, of course, but preferring to occupy Sir William and Lady Vernon Harcourt's stand at Whitehall, where Miss Fetridge and Julian and I would have an opportunity to rest and lunch in the intervals of waiting, I promptly gave the Buckingham Palace tickets to two guests of mine. It did not occur to me until afterwards what an abominably improper thing I had done.

Later I explained this shocking breach of etiquette as best I could to the Prince, and he said that he had wondered as he had passed the Buckingham Palace stand and looked for me why he couldn't see me where he had expected me to be.

Notwithstanding this social blunder on my part, I enjoyed myself to the utmost. I wouldn't for anything on earth have missed the piping Highlanders marching up and down Whitehall, while we were waiting for the royal procession. The music of bagpipes always had the power to thrill me to the marrow. One of the greatest men and smallest officers, General Lord Roberts, received an ovation second only to that of the Queen, while the tallest man in the British Army, Colonel Oswald Ames, being astride a charger and therefore looking no more imposing than any one else, passed without creating any great excitement.

The Buckingham Palace garden party, which took place after the procession, and to which I was invited, owed its unusual brilliance that year to the presence of the princes of India, who were literally covered and weighed down with magnificent jewels. These impressive, dignified Hindus proved to be too much for the curiosity of the English ladies present. Had they been manikins in a shop they would not have been more thoroughly inspected. One could not help wondering, as one watched these women of the British nobility walk up to these bejeweled Brahmans and stare them out of countenance, what such sensitive, highly bred princes must think of the ways of so-called civilization.

At this garden party the royal family and their court walked from the palace to the marquee, bowing to the guests standing on either side of the path and occasionally stopping to speak to this or that individual. This royal party included the Empress Frederick and was headed by the Prince of Wales. When I speak of the Prince of Wales in this history,

I am always referring to the one who afterwards became King Edward VII, the only Prince of Wales with whom I was acquainted. While this royal procession was in progress my friends and I, not being of the pushing sort, were continually crowded out of our places into others farther down the line. At last one of the men of our party said that if the Prince continued to see us appear and disappear at every few steps, he would begin to think he was the victim of a hallucination. In the end, however, we were rewarded for our meekly submitting to being shoved about, by having the Prince and Princess of Wales and the Empress Frederick stop and speak to us.

When that London season, during which we occupied the house of the Duchesse de Bassano overlooking Kensington Gardens and the Bayswater end of the Serpentine, was completed, Queen Victoria commanded me to sing for her at Osborne House. Tosti, composer of the famous "Good-bye," was my accompanist. My first number, I must admit, was rather trembling. My admiration for Queen Victoria, both as a sovereign and as a woman, was such that, although, as a rule, I have little respect for names, position, and possessions, I was so filled with emotion when I learned that I was to sing for her with only fifteen feet between us that my self-confidence was affected. However, I soon regained command of myself.

The Queen was most charming to me, and at the end of the concert I found that the face which had such a stern and almost surly expression in repose was completely transformed by her smile. She conferred the Jubilee medal upon me, which, according to report, was distributed by bucketfuls to men, but given to very few women.

After the presentation of the medal, Lord Edward Pelham Clinton, Master of the Queen's Household, uncle of the present Duke of Newcastle and a friend of mine, told me that Queen Victoria had asked that I sign her autograph book at Osborne, which I did. Then, upon my return to London I wrote Lord Edward the customary note thanking the Queen for the decoration, and adding that I wished I had sung more to my own taste and consequently in a way more worthy of the great sovereign to whom I was singing, but that I had been overcome by emotion and awe. Evidently the note pleased her because she asked Lord Edward's permission to add it to her autograph collection.

From London we returned to Paris for just the length of time necessary to prepare for my second visit to Bayreuth, this time accompanied by Julian.

The previous winter, while in Paris, I had begun to study Wagner's operas in German with the chief *répétiteur* at Bayreuth and Frau Cosima's right-hand man. Anton Seidl had begged me to learn Sieglinde in "Die Walküre," calling it the bridge between such rôles as Eva and Elizabeth and the heavier Wagner rôles. Previously I had only sung "Lohengrin" and "Tannhäuser" in Italian, and I wanted to add these and Sieglinde to my repertoire in German.

It might be interesting to note here that I studied Sieglinde for two years before I considered I had sufficient command of the rôle to trust myself to sing it in public. The character and the music affected me so much that I could not sing certain phrases without choking, and I knew that until I could conquer this I could never reach or convince my audience. This vivid impression of, and emotional sympathy with, the character to be sung always came to me with the first reading of the words and music of any opera and formed the basis of any future interpretation. But having

175

registered this keynote of the character, I had to rise above sympathetic emotion—I am here revealing what were my steps towards the accomplishment of a fundamental, serious operatic interpretation—and become a cool, calm, clear medium through which the soul of the character being sung might flow out to my hearers.

Before my arrival in Bayreuth that summer I heard that Jean de Reszke had been outraged by receiving as soon as he reached Bayreuth, a message from Frau Wagner telling him she would be delighted to give him an "audition" at the theater any morning. This, to the prince of tenors—perhaps the greatest and best known and most adored tenor of his period.

When, therefore, after hearing of Jean de Reszke's experience, I got a message through Mr. Seidl that Frau Wagner was very anxious to meet me, I sent her word that I would pay my respects to her any afternoon, but that as I was not strong I was never allowed to go out in the morning. After my operation, a London season and the general state of exhaustion that followed, I did not feel in a conciliatory mood.

Frau Wagner let me know that she would

be delighted to receive me at Wahnfried on the following afternoon about four o'clock. When I presented an appearance, she took me at once into a little salon, as though there were no question of hearing me sing. We had a short chat, and then she said:

"Am I not to hear you at all? I have heard so much about you and am *most* anxious to hear you sing."

Of course I replied that I had had a very strenuous season and had not been well, that I had just arrived from a long journey and did not feel much like singing, but that if she wished me to I would do so.

I had refused to pay this visit unless Mr. Seidl accompanied me. He was extremely amused at the whole episode and seconded me in every way.

When Frau Wagner asked me what I would sing, some devil must have prompted me, for I replied that I would sing Schumann's "Widmung," knowing the hideous feud that had existed between Schumann and Wagner.

Frau Wagner put on the most bewildered air and said to my accompanist: "Schumann, Schumann, have you any works of Schumann?" On being told "No," she asked me if I knew anything of the master's that I would sing to her, and I said I would sing anything. She looked through the operas I knew and chose one of the most difficult phrases for any one whose voice is not absolutely at her command, the one in the duet between the two women in the second act of "Lohengrin," beginning, *"Du ärmst' kannst du wohl nie ermessen."* I was in rather good voice, I think, and she seemed to be extremely pleased, and at the termination, young Wagnerians of both sexes rained down from various balconies surrounding the central hall where I sang. Before I left, Austrian archdukes bent before her, kissing her hand as though she were royalty, and treating her with the greatest, deepest deference—still another proof that whether you deserve it·or not, it is not a bad thing to cultivate a good opinion of yourself.

Frau Cosima was neither beautiful, lovable, gracious, tactful, nor fitted to add any luster to the interpretations of her husband's operas agreed upon before his death. But, from a few years after his death until the Great War, just because she thought well of herself the world did likewise; and she ruled the greatest and most historic institution in the musical world —the Bayreuth Festival.

The following season in London, Frau Wag-

VALLOMBROSA ESTATE.

ner was present when Wagner's entire "Ring" was sung, led by the great Mottl.

One unforgettable incident of the particular festival of 1897 was the manner in which Siegfried Wagner led "Parsifal." In the last act the orchestra and chorus went entirely to pieces, and the performance had to be stopped and a new start made. Nor was this the only flaw in the performance that year. On my first visit in 1886 the artists still respected Wagner's wishes and submerged themselves in the music drama. In 1897 they rushed to the footlights and sang to the audience. In 1886 Bayreuth was a temple of art surrounded by beautiful woods; in 1897 it was an opera house surrounded by enormous beer saloons.

The Prince and Princess of Wales attended the festival that year and were entranced with my beloved Peeny, who was hardly more than a puppy. At the restaurant where we often met, the Princess always stopped me to play with Peeny.

From Bayreuth we journeyed to Italy and Vallombrosa. The preceding summer, in order to have a place of our own, we had rented a most charming and convenient little house from my sister-in-law. It was really two peasant houses made into one. But this summer, following our Bayreuth visit, we took a parish house, the erstwhile home of a local priest, with a big terrace overlooking the valley and the Arno gleaming in the distance. To it was attached a little country chapel where Mass was held every Sunday.

We used this house only as a place in which to eat and sleep. In that perfect country one spent one's waking hours out-of-doors and in the woods of Vallombrosa. On the clear, beautiful, moonlit Italian nights we would sit on the great terrace in that gentle silence which was broken only by distant voices singing a snatch of song, or the occasional barking of a dog.

V

THE winter following my second visit to Bayreuth I was obliged to give up singing in America for two reasons. The first was that the effort I had made to sing at the Diamond Jubilee so soon after my operation had made it dangerous for me to undertake the strain of an American operatic season. The second was that the contract Mr. Grau was able to offer me that year, although it included a large increase in my fee, contained clauses superimposed by the machinations of a singer already engaged to which I could not bring myself to agree.

It had always been my custom, when it came to signing my contracts, to consider the rights of other singers in the matter of rôles as well as the difficulties in casting that confront any director in making up his season's repertoire, and I had always tried to "play fair." I had even gone so far in one case as to relinquish my exclusive right to a rôle in order that a rival artist might sing it, believing that it would be both cowardly and unfair for me to refuse to submit to comparison, however odious. Unfortunately, others had not these same operatic ethics; and after reading the only contract Mr. Grau could offer me that season, I told him I preferred to spend the winter in Paris.

The following spring, that of 1898, I went to London for my usual season of opera there. One of the greatest pleasures of my London seasons was the visit the Prince of Wales paid me in my dressing room every night that I sang. This was always preceded by his equerry coming to me before the performance and asking at what time during the evening it would be most convenient for me to receive His Royal Highness, as the Prince, in his infinite tact, realized that no matter how great an honor an interview with royalty may be, it is also a strain.

Another king, without a throne, lacked the scrupulous courtesy and breeding always evinced by the Prince of Wales, and got well snubbed for his manners, although the snubbing was wholly unintentional on my part. This prince was far from an honor to his rank and distinctly boorish into the bargain.

We were doing the "Ring" that season in London, and one evening, during one of the prolonged entr'actes of "Die Walküre," Plançon came to my door and said, just before he opened it, "Madame Eames, —— wishes to be presented to you."

And I, knowing only the courtesy and tact of royalty that behaved as royalty should, never dreamed that Plançon was not alone, and called emphatically in French, "As for that one, no, no, no!"

There was a dead silence, and I observed that a friend who was with me that night and sat facing the door of my dressing room, seemed horribly embarrassed. Afterwards, when I asked the reason, she told me that this prince had been just behind Plançon during the little scene and had heard my answer.

I was of course confounded, and immediately wrote Plançon an apology for having placed him in such an uncomfortable position, and concluded with: "But how could I imagine that a gentleman who did not know me would have dared to present himself at my dressing room without having asked previously if it would be agreeable for me to receive him?"

The next evening that I sang I decided to tell the Prince of Wales the exact circumstances in order to confute any garbled version of the episode that he might hear. I began calmly and with great restraint to relate the details, when suddenly my feelings were too much for me and, throwing discretion to the winds, I burst out indignantly, "Anyway, he's a dirty boy, and I'm glad I did it."

And the Prince answered with a little laugh, "He *is* a dirty boy, and I am glad you did it, too."

This was the season when we occupied Lady Eardley's house, in Lancaster Gate, just one street back of the Duchess of Bassano's, which we had occupied the previous summer, and when I sang for the first time one of the most difficult rôles ever written for a soprano voice, Ero in Mancinelli's "Ero e Leandro." Mancinelli's opera is a melodious, erudite work containing many passages of great beauty and charm, but the music of the principal rôles does not spare its interpreter. For instance, the climax of the great aria is built up by a repetition of the same group of notes in an ascending scale, requiring endless breath and power of resistance. Saleza was the Leandro, and the opera was very well staged.

This was the season when Queen Victoria again asked for a private performance of "Romeo and Juliet." Only this time, when Jean de Reszke had a repetition of that strange and sudden illness that had been responsible for my making my operatic bow to Her Majesty in the secondary rôle of Micaela in "Carmen" years before, Saleza was substituted as Romeo and I appeared before the Queen as Juliet after all.

Lord Edward Pelham Clinton, still Master of the Queen's Household, told me afterwards that before the performance Queen Victoria had particularly enjoined him to instruct the court that they were not to regard her cessation of applause as the customary signal; that, as she was a great admirer of mine, they were to continue to applaud even though she were obliged to stop.

A magnificent room—I judged it to be one of the smaller reception rooms—had been temporarily converted into a dressing room for me, with the aid of a great dressing table and necessary toilet adjuncts. Its walls were adorned with beautiful pictures by Van Dyck, Vanloo, Rubens and others, and I was so busy looking at them that I had great difficulty in tearing myself away in order to dress. The light from many candles instead of the modern electric lights served me when I came to put on my make-up.

Candlelight is so much more agreeable than

185

electric light. I shall never forget my introduction to the latter. It took place in the dining room on the top floor of the then new Auditorium Hotel in Chicago in 1891, long before the day of roof gardens. The bulbs were unshaded, and when I came in for dinner every one of their tiny blazing wires seemed to leap at me and burn itself into my brain and I became so nauseated that I had to leave. During the remainder of my stay I dined in my rooms with shaded lights.

The night of the command "Romeo and Juliet" performance a small forest of palms and plants served as a bridge between the stage and the raised platform upon which sat the Queen and her court. As this mass of green completely concealed the orchestra, we could look directly at our royal audience, who seemed framed in flowers. The effect was decidedly wonderful.

In addition to the perfect setting it was one of those exalted performances where every one does better than one's best. That it so happened was a great joy to me, because I always wished to give the finest of which I was capable whenever I had to sing for any one so great and so good as Queen Victoria.

As a very special honor I was invited to sup

afterwards with the royal family. This necessitated my getting out of my costume and make-up post haste and donning an elaborate evening gown and dressing my hair with great care, albeit hastily enough, instead of slipping into the usual simple gown and tucking my hair up comfortably. When at last I was ready, I was taken to make my bow to the Queen.

She received me with one of her beautiful smiles and said: "You were not afraid tonight, I'm sure." referring to the Osborne incident and my letter thereupon. "You were very wonderful."

I was terribly moved, as I always was in her presence, and have no recollection of my answer, except that it caused her to burst into sudden and most hearty laughter.

It may be considered a wonderful honor to sup with the royal family in this fashion, but it is much more comfortable to go home, slip into a teagown and have a cup of bouillon and a bite of something, unabashed by the presence of crowned heads. Therefore, after I had nibbled a sandwich, I sought out Lord Edward and implored him to get me away and out of the castle as quickly as possible.

The Queen had instructed her first lady in

waiting to see that the royal gift to me was an unusually beautiful one. And it cannot be said that her wish in the matter was not fully carried out, for Lord Edward placed in my hands a golden angel standing on a huge diamond and holding a scroll in her outstretched hands on which was inscribed in rubies, "Victoria R. I." Her outspread wings were set solidly with diamonds and rubies; her girdle was of diamonds, with a big diamond in the center, and her coronet was composed of the same stones. My first gift from Her Majesty, which had been presented after the performance of the substituted "Carmen" two years before, had been a pin about an inch and a half wide with her monogram, "V.R.I.," in rubies and diamonds, surmounted by a crown.

Both of these mementos were burned in the fire that, as I have already stated, destroyed all my possessions as they were *en route* to America during the War. I do not think I have ever quite recovered from the shock of this loss, but in view of the horrors that were taking place in the world at that time I was ashamed to utter a word of complaint at the destruction of a few earthly possessions, no matter how valuable.

In the summer of 1898 the blue prints for

the house we had planned to build in Italy were approved by us, but the actual construction was turned over to our architect, while we went to America for the season of 1898-99. This architect left a master of the works who remained on the spot, living in a room at the farm made for him as comfortable as possible. Later we remained until November in the completed and comfortable house. This made me realize the overpowering loneliness and chill this poor man must have endured. He did, in fact, have an attack of erysipelas, during which he was cared for by an "orca" or sort of witch or magic doctor, who used incantations as well as herbs for his cure. It was all very primitive, for the peasantry was plunged in the darkest ignorance. Once when a cow died we were told in strong Tuscan dialect, upon asking the cause of her death, that the local veterinary had pronounced that "she wished to die."

In this period of high wages it might be interesting to note that the skilled stonecutters who worked on our house were paid from two to two and a half francs a day, while the ordinary masons were paid a franc. They began work at six in the morning and stopped at six at night, with an interval of from an hour and

a half to two hours in the middle of the day
for a siesta. They lived in a small village at
the foot of the mountain, and it took them
three quarters of an hour to reach our place.

The stone for the house was quarried on our
own land, but the sand for the plaster had to
be carted a long distance. We had planned a
replica of a medieval castle, and began with
one wing and a tower. This was as far as we
ever got, because even this was so colossal that
we were lost in it.

The tower was over sixty-five feet high.
The entrance hall, which also served as a living
room, was eighty feet long and thirty-five
feet wide and two stories high, with a staircase
and gallery and the roof for a ceiling. The
foundations were six feet thick, and in escarp-
ment. The finish was an exact copy of that
of the Bargello in Florence. It was of chest-
nut, which had been oiled and lightly stained
before the decorations, in very faded colors,
were added. The walls were painted in soft
dull colors, the medieval process known as in
tempera being used—in which the paint was
mixed with milk. It was months before the
all-pervading smell of milk disappeared.

Our workmen were, of course, all Italians

who had been born to this type of construction and decoration. Others, without the tradition in their blood, could never have reproduced such a perfect illusion of ancient workmanship.

We planted lilies and jasmine and honeysuckle about our castle, and on the great terrace before it we put an old-fashioned fountain and pots of orange and lemon trees. Alas, these tropical shrubs died after a season. Being situated between two mountains that created a sort of gigantic draught, our place was cool almost to chilliness, even in the summer, and did not afford our poor orange trees the climate in which they might flourish. We had, however, a wealth of flowers of a hardier sort that reached great proportions: geraniums filled the beds surrounding the fountains and on lower and more protected terraces, pinks, verbena, lemon verbena, and heliotrope blossomed in great profusion. By pure coincidence our young gardener was named Faust—called familiarly Faustino—and we had a young linen maid named Aïda. They met at our place and married, he bringing her back to Campigliono to live. The following year a child was born, whom, in order to keep up the operatic tradition, they named Rigoletto, which being translated means literally "little fool."

Across the valley was the forest of Vallombrosa, affording us a beautiful view of wooded slopes as well as being a mecca for excursions. Behind us rose a mountain, the ridge of which provided a rough high road or trail, called Strada Maremmana, for the shepherds and their flocks. As the seasons varied they could be seen making their leisurely way to the lowlands or toiling up to the highlands, as the case might be.

After returning from a two-hour to three-hour walk that might have taken us through the woods as far as the Consuma, which lies on the direct road to Casentino, celebrated for many of the bloody fights of the Guelphs and the Ghibellines, we used to picnic on this ridge in the evening. The period of the harvest and hunter's moon, when the sun sets almost simultaneously with the rising of the moon, was one we particularly loved for these picnics, as it enabled us to stroll home by bright moonlight after supper.

Our very dear friends, the Boits, at whose home I had met Henry James in my girlhood, were our inseparable companions on these jaunts. They had bought a most enchanting farm not far from us, which they had converted into a comfortable and delightful house. It had formerly been the property of the monks of Vallombrosa, and one of their farms, and all the rooms were erstwhile cells. The Boits had managed to make it over into a dwelling place without destroying its original character, and had left unchanged the beautiful great terrace on which the monks had had their vegetable garden. This terrace was divided up by paths made of rough, flat, irregular stones, into rose beds which were a mass of bloom the whole summer. In the center of the garden surrounded by walls three feet high was a great octagonal basin from which rose a single jet of water. This fountain had served the monks as a source of water in former years.

In the summer when we drew up the plans for Torre di Campiglioni, Mr. Grau came to me to assure me of my engagement for the following season in America and asked me, as was his custom, what new opera I should like to sing that year.

I answered, "Aïda!"

He threw up his hands in despair. "Why," he cried, "choose an opera in which you have to be a Negress? No one will be able to see what you look like. Why not choose sure successes? 'Aïda' has never drawn in America, no matter how great a cast I gave it."

I insisted, however, telling him that the idea that I must do "Aïda" had become an obsession with me. In the end he acceded to my desire, and assured me that he would give it every chance, with new scenery, new costumes for the chorus and full rehearsals.

He was as good as his word, and saw to it that the chorus and orchestra were rehearsed as carefully as though it were a new opera, and that the scenery was refurbished—although scenery in those days was not looked upon as the most important part of opera.

To secure the proper make-up for Aïda I combined the formula Sarah Bernhardt used in creating the peculiarly beautiful color of her Cleopatra, and of which Mrs. Grau had told me, with certain ingredients of my own discovery, the composition of which I have never told and never shall! The result was an Aïda darker than Sarah's lovely Cleopatra, rather the dull copper color of the North American Indian, and one who was—I can say it, since she bore no resemblance to Emma Eames— very, very beautiful. I completed this make-up by abandoning the unsightly cotton arm pieces worn by previous Aïdas and painting my arms, face and neck with my famous preparation.

During the rehearsals I gave no hint to any one of the interpretation I had planned for Aïda. I had worked it out in secret and, as it seemed to me to be very audacious, I quite trembled and wondered if I should have the *aplomb* to carry it out once before my audience. I had created Aïda as I did my other rôles—I say "created" because, although "Aïda" was an old opera, in keeping faith with my rule of never attending an opera in which I might have to sing, I had never seen the rôle portrayed for fear of adopting, unconsciously, some other singer's interpretation—without the aid of a looking-glass, having relied upon the mirror of my imagination as the truer reflector.

Just before the performance the assistant manager came to my dressing room to see my costumes—as indeed many of my comrades did on my first nights, for my costumes were considered always so beautiful and so correct. When he saw me in my Aïda make-up he exclaimed, "No one would ever know you. How you have transformed yourself!"

This remark gave me the courage of my planned interpretation, and I dared to act

Aïda as the mirror of my imagination had shown her to me, a little passionate, panting savage, albeit a princess. I was told that as Aïda was a prima donna's rôle, a seat on the throne was always provided for her beside Amneris. This seemed to me idiotic, as one was in ignorance of Aïda's royal origin. I therefore insisted upon sitting on the steps at the feet of Amneris, the slave's proper attitude.

We sang "Aïda" for the first time in Buffalo with de Marchi as Rhadames. Then we presented this opera in New York, and it took the town by storm. The subsequent popularity of the work is too well known for me to comment upon. I have sometimes wondered, as I saw it become a veritable war horse, the old reliable that has inaugurated opera season after opera season in New York and Chicago, if to-day the opera goers praise or blame me most for its revival.

It might be well to mention that perhaps some of the credit for the startling success of "Aïda" was due to the inspiration I always derived from the American audiences. The American public, open-hearted, responsive and keenly alive and eager to hear its favorites, not only made me feel that it was glad to see me do well, which is always a help, but brought

Photograph by Aimé Dupont

AS AIDA

with it an atmosphere of enthusiasm which communicated its vibrations to me.

Those who did not hear me sing in America never really heard me. In England the audiences do not meet the artists halfway. Years of self-repression and direction prevent them from letting themselves go, at least at first, and I always dreaded the first act, during which I had to rouse them. They were very friendly and willing to be moved, and once moved very enthusiastic, but, as I said before, they do not meet one halfway. And in consequence the London season, coming as it did immediately after the long and exciting one in America, was always a strain.

That season of the sensational revival of "Aïda" the entire company made a continent-wide tour, which began in Canada at Montreal, went south to New Orleans and then west by way of San Antonio and Los Angeles to San Francisco. Calvé, Sembrich, Sybil Sanderson and myself were among those who carried the burden of the principal feminine rôles on that trip.

Julian was in very poor health that year and unable to accompany me. The best doctors of London and Paris had been unable to discover the cause of his illness; and at last, in desperation, I had written to his cousin, an eminent physician of Philadelphia, Dr. George McClellan, asking for his help on our arrival in New York. Dr. McClellan took charge of the case, quieted my anxiety by assuring me that Julian would have the best of care during my absence, and told me, if I really wanted to hasten the cure, to write Julian a cheerful letter every day which contained no suggestion of depression or worry about his condition; that that would be the best possible tonic for him. And, acting upon Dr. McClellan's instructions, I wrote my husband daily volumes about the innumerable amusing, entertaining and novel things that happened on our coast-to-coast journey.

In Montreal, in order to have a place big enough to accommodate the audience, we gave the performance in the skating rink. The opera in which I sang was "Tannhäuser," with Dippel as the hero and myself as Elizabeth. Just before the performance the weather, which had been doubtful all day, turned to a downpour. The roof of the rink, although really not in bad shape, might have been tighter than it was. And Dippel, egged on by Walter Damrosch, began the series of Weber and Fields jokes that followed us to the Pacific Coast by appearing in the wings holding a huge cotton umbrella, which in conjunction with his Tannhäuser costume, put us into a hilarious mood from which we found it difficult to recover for the serious work of the evening.

Our experiences on this tour were extremely varied. In Atlanta, Georgia, the raising of the curtain revealed one of the loveliest sights that I have ever witnessed. All the beautiful women of Atlanta—and it is famed for its beautiful women—seemed to be present in their most exquisite gowns, and each held a bouquet in her lap. It was more like an enchanted flower garden than an audience.

From this heavenly vision, we descended to things less lovely; in short, to the flying cockroaches in those Southern hotel dining rooms. Not knowing what they were at first, I called the attention of the waiter to these insects, and asked him how there happened to be so many humming birds in the room. He was hugely amused and with a fat Negro laugh answered: "But dem ain't no hummin' birds; dem's flyin' cockroaches!"

We seemed to strike a convention in every city of our itinerary. I remember in Houston, Texas—where we sang "Lohengrin" in the big hall used for such conventions—the walls of our dressing rooms were covered with gruesome sketches of coffins, skulls and crossbones, all reminiscences of the previous show. Although Mr. Grau's managers used every care and precaution, oftener than not we were compelled to put up with the most primitive accommodations in our dressing rooms. The day before we were due in Houston that city's chief hotel burned to the ground, and upon our arrival we had to pack ourselves into a smaller one. I came off rather better than most, for Miss Fetridge harangued the loiterers in the hotel lobby and begged some one of them to show the Southern chivalry for which his state was famous by giving up his room to me. This was done immediately, I must confess, and Southern chivalry vindicated its reputation.

However, the enthusiasm and understanding of our audiences more than compensated for any inconveniences or discomforts along the way. And some incident was always taking place in the various towns to brighten our stay for us. One evening in Buffalo, as Sybil Sanderson, Miss Fetridge, and I were sitting down to dinner in Sybil's room—again on account of overcrowding we had to eat in our bedrooms—a pale-faced young man walked into the room. Thinking him a reporter, I immediately told him to leave, but instead he advanced toward us and murmured that he wanted a drink. By this time I was thoroughly incensed at the intrusion and rising, took him by the shoulders, marched him to the door and thrust him out into the hall, where he tottered away to his room. Sybil, being very human and filled with curiosity, rushed to the door to see who he might be and where he went. She discovered that he was not a reporter after all, but a young man celebrating his wedding journey by getting into the most violent state of intoxication. Almost immediately he emerged from his room and went downstairs for that famous drink for which he had asked us and of which, certainly, he had no need. And Sybil and I, rushing across the hall, peeped into the room he had left and discovered that the poor little bride, who was dissolved in tears, had had no dinner and was in despair over the antics of this remarkable bridegroom.

At last we arrived in California, in my case, in San Francisco. I made my San Francisco début in "Tannhäuser," and of course later sang in the "Nozze di Figaro" with Sembrich.

It was at this last performance that the brother of a dear friend of mine, Dr. Tevis, gave me one of the most charming surprises that it had ever been my good fortune to receive in my career. He stationed people with huge bouquets of roses and carnations in the front row and the boxes on either side of the stage, and at a signal after the great aria in the third act, "Dove sono," these flowers were thrown to me in a shower. For a moment the air seemed filled with roses. My emotion and delight at this least of his many kindnesses during our friendship can more readily be imagined than described.

Not long after this, calamity descended upon the opera company, and one after another the various members succumbed to California grippe. I was the last victim, falling ill about a week before I was to sing "Aïda." As no one expected I should be able to go through with this performance, Mr. Grau announced as much to the San Francisco guarantors, and these gentlemen immediately insisted upon a doctor's certificate. No doubt their demand was prompted by the strange rumor to the effect that Grau was not letting his star singers appear whenever he felt he could substitute cheaper ones. Nothing could have been more naïve to any one who knows anything about operatic contracts. An operatic contract calls for a certain number of performances which must be offered to the artist within the terms and conditions of the contract, and if not offered must be paid for as guaranteed. The "economy" therefore of which he was accused would have been quite the reverse, as he would have had to pay two people instead of one.

When the guarantors insisted upon my physician signing a certificate stating that I was unable to sing, Mr. Grau said—and I was deeply touched when told of it—

"Gentlemen, I will exact it if you wish; but I know two things about Madame Eames: the first is that if she says she cannot sing, it is because she really cannot; and the second, if she is unable to sing it is through no fault of her own."

However, I heard that the San Franciscans were expressing a losing confidence in the company, which is always the death knell of any season; and I decided that it was incumbent upon me to make a superhuman effort to sing "Aïda." A bad bronchial attack was one symptom of my grippe and this made it impossible for me to speak. In fact, to try to speak one word brought on terrible coughing fits.

But I discovered upon trying my singing voice —one sings above one's speaking voice—that it seemed in good condition. Therefore I risked the "Aïda" performance and, except for one note, I never sang better. But afterwards my heart gave out from the strain of the responsibility and anxiety, and I was ill for days. However, I never regretted the enormous effort, for the day was saved for Grau and the people's faith in him restored.

San Francisco in those days was as different from the present one as the modern New York is unlike that of 1891. Its society was simple, limited in number and charming and those I saw seemed like one large joyous family.

Dr. Tevis gave me a delightful party at the Bohemian Club. The banquet hall was garlanded with flowers and the little supper tables decorated with poinsettias. The guests, being in truly festal mood, made a real celebration of it. On another occasion I was shown the original Chinatown, at least that part of it that could be decently visited, and afterwards was grateful for the opportunity, as its charm and Oriental character had completely vanished when I visited it again in later years after the earthquake.

The town made the opera season an occasion for festival, and the Palace Hotel—the same Palace Hotel to which we went upon our arrival from China years before—was the scene of many dinners before the opera and innumerable parties afterwards. This hotel was built around a large, roofed-in courtyard, a true Spanish type of patio. In honor of the opera season one half of this courtyard had been converted into a palm grove, carpeted with beautiful Oriental rugs and warmed here and there with braziers of blazing charcoal. Two Chinese, in the colorful costumes of their country, were stationed at the doors to admit the guests.

As an additional courtesy to the opera company, John Mackay, president of the Commercial Cable Company, put the cables at our disposal, in order that we might send any message we wished to our friends. I looked upon this as a mere gracious matter of form, until one day Mr. Mackay called upon me and told me that the other members of the company were sending volumes all over the world, and begged me to do likewise. I immediately complied, and sent three or four reckless cables to different friends. One of them told me afterwards that she received a long cable from me filled with "ifs" and "ands," she thought I must have taken leave of my senses.

Upon our return to New York, I sang Ero in "Ero e Leandro" and my beloved Sieglinde in "Die Walküre," with Lili Lehmann as Brünhilde, Schumann-Heink as Frika, Van Rooy as Wotan, and Van Dyke as Siegmund, Anton Seidl conducting. I dressed Sieglinde in sand color, as the traditional white costumes worn by others who played the part had always seemed to me too startling. I felt that Sieglinde should seem to melt into the dim, eerie light of most of her scenes.

It was about this time that Frau Wagner, who had often asked me previously to sing at Bayreuth, again sent me a message by one of her great admirers, begging me to sing the following season at the great Wagnerian festival, assuring me that she knew how to treat an artist and that I should receive every consideration. Having heard tales of the way she treated artists, particularly Jean de Reszke, I told this intermediary that I did not care to place myself at her mercy. I added further that, since singers only went to Bayreuth for prestige, and in order to be able to demand a bigger fee in America, and as I felt I needed neither more prestige nor a larger fee, I saw

As Ero in "Ero e Leandro"

As Sieglinde in "Die Walküre"

no reason for subjecting myself to the commercialized Bayreuth of 1900 that bore no resemblance to its original.

We played the "Magic Flute" that year, with Sembrich as the Queen of the Night, myself as Pamina and—to give some idea of the status of the rest of the cast—the great Ternina as the first Demoiselle. Mozart's opera, for which the prices of admission were raised, was very carefully prepared and rehearsed, but we who took part in it called it disrespectfully, "the four-ring circus."

Towards the end of the nineties, during one of the seasons when I did not sing in America, I created at Monte Carlo, the rôle of Ghisèle, in the posthumous work of that name by César Franck. It was a tiring, difficult, ungrateful rôle—the opera was never successful enough to become part of any operatic repertoire—and at the end of the first performance I returned to my dressing room, flung myself into a chair and said to my rather green French maid, "Oh, Josephine, I am so tired. Undress me." *"Je crois bien, madame,"* she answered, *"après avoir crié comme ça pendant toute une soirée."* ("I should think you would be, madame, after shouting like that a whole evening.")

This fatigue, so delightfully accounted for by my maid, should have been a warning signal; but I had, in my concentration on my work, a bad habit of disregarding signals. My only existence was in my music. The events in the outside world made no impression upon me. The other day some one asked some question about the Boer War, and I answered, without thinking how it sounded, "Oh, I was so terribly busy at the time that I didn't notice it." And the absurd part of that statement was its perfect truth.

The habit of becoming so tremendously absorbed in my work, combined with the overstimulating climate of New York, soon began to tell on me, and the week before the first performance of the "Magic Flute" brought me to a breakdown.

My breakdowns were not the collapses of most people, but a rebellion of my nerves which caused all my muscles to contract spasmodically, particularly those of my throat. The crisis of this one came on in a performance of the "Nozze di Figaro," when feeling this contraction overtaking me, I was seized with panic at the idea of being alone on the stage during the singing of the great aria beginning, "Dove sono." I sent for Mancinelli, who was conducting that evening, and told him what had happened; and when he saw my face tears came into his eyes and he said, "Not only shall you not sing that aria, but we'll stop the opera, if you want us to."

I answered: "Oh, no; I think I can manage if other people are on the stage with me."

And I did manage, although I was only able barely to sketch the part.

The next day I said very calmly to my beloved Miss Fetridge: "I know how to sing, and the doctor says there is nothing the matter with my voice. Therefore, my inability to sing last night can only be accounted for by the fact that I must be insane." And then I asked her to send for the great nerve specialist and alienist, Dr. George Jacoby.

Dr. Jacoby came and, after hearing the whole story, said: "But, my dear child, will you have no mercy on yourself? You have driven yourself beyond your limit of endurance. That is all. You must have a complete rest."

But I told him that before I could rest I must sing in those four performances of the "Magic Flute" for which Mr. Grau was depending upon me; and that no matter what happened to me afterwards, I must not leave him in the lurch.

Dr. Jacoby considered this, and then began his years of intelligent care of me by telling me that he would agree to only one thing, and that was that should he, on the day of the performance, feel that I was able to go through an evening on the stage without injury to myself, he would consent to my singing. And if he did not think so, and if I had not responded to treatment as he hoped, and was not able to sing, Mr. Grau would have to be left in the lurch, "Magic Flute" or no "Magic Flute."

At last both Mr. Grau and myself agreed to this wise ultimatum, and keeping any hint of the true state of affairs from the public, I lay in a darkened room, letting my brain and nerves relax, taking a few simple remedies and no drugs until the day of the general rehearsal of the "Magic Flute," when I was allowed to sing. Each of the four performances of the opera was preceded by this same treatment, including quiet rest in the darkened room.

There was a great clamor that spring, after the presentation of the "Magic Flute" for a last performance of "Faust," and Mr. Grau begged me to appear one last time that season as Marguerite. But I simply could not. I had sung the rôle so many evenings that winter, in spite of my fatigue, that I was certain that the memory of the effort I had had to make, in addition to my weakened condition, would make it impossible for me to get through it. The only thing that made the "Magic Flute" possible for me was the fact that I was appearing in it for the first time and it had no painful associations.

At the conclusion of this season Dr. Jacoby sent me away for an eighteen months' rest.

As I was not strong enough to superintend the moving of the furniture we had bought the year before into our new house in Vallombrosa, I remained in Paris while Julian went on ahead to get everything in readiness for me. In what seemed to me an incredibly short time he sent for me, and upon my arrival at Vallombrosa I found that, as the big house was as yet uninhabitable, he had had a cosy little apartment prepared for us in an adjacent farmhouse of ours.

Before the summer was over, however, we were established in our own home, Torre di Campiglioni. Here, in a country where the siesta was a national habit, it was easy for me to do nothing but sleep and rest and give the overtired nerves of my throat a chance to recuperate.

All summer long I was literally buried in dogs. My little Peeny had had four beautiful puppies, and the first-born, much larger than his mother, a splendid, golden-brown dachshund whom I called Haensel, or my Golden Knight, struggled to get to me even before his eyes were open. Peeny seemed to have passed the love she had for me on to him twofold. We kept one other puppy of this litter, whom we named Tekel. His specialty was watching the builders at work, and every day you might see him seated at some strategic point keeping his eye on the construction of the terrace and grounds.

In addition to the dachshunds we had two pedigreed Scotch deerhounds, a gift to Julian. And one of these deerhounds, named Onward, and Haensel, never would let me out of their sight. Even during my afternoon siesta they had to be with me. Being little more than puppies, at first it was thought that they would be noisy and disturb me, and they were turned over to one of the servants for safe-keeping during my daily nap. But they always escaped, and flew to my bedroom door to sniff and scratch and whine until they were admitted. At last I decided that they couldn't be noisier in the room than at the door, and let them stay with me. They showed their appreciation of this concession by keeping still as mice each afternoon until I awakened.

Every time I sat down at least four dogs plunged forward and tried to sit on me, and I never could convince Onward, the deerhound, that he was not a lap dog. Haensel carried his devotion to me even to the point of insisting upon being with me when I practiced. He would rush up and jump and demand to be taken up while I was standing at the piano. At last one day I picked him up impatiently, and put him down hard on the top of the piano with the command: "Stay there!" And he did stay there, and furthermore every day thereafter insisted upon staying there. He would lie with his head on his paws, his eyes never moving from me, the whole time I sang.

Many years afterwards I had another dachshund, who loathed anything like practicing, but was enchanted by melody and never protested against even my highest note. When I sang scales or any other form of vocalises she would howl in anguish, and sustained notes caused a paroxysm during which she tried to

213

sing literally the same note and succeeded! One could not criticize her musical taste!

We remained in Italy during that summer and fall of 1899 and the whole of 1900. Our dear friends, and afterward neighbors, the Boits, came to Vallombrosa in the summer of 1899 and bought and rebuilt the house I have described previously, called Cernitoio. The next summer many delightful people came to Vallombrosa and the Saltino from Sicily and the vicinity of Naples, as Vallombrosa is a very fashionable mountain resort for Italians. Diplomats marooned in Rome for the hot months found it a relief to run up to the mountains by the funicular railway for a breath of cool air. As we had a delightful house, with plenty of guest rooms and an excellent chef—the food offered by the summer hotels beggared description—our home became a rendezvous for all these people, who came to visit and often remained to buy or build. It was not long before we were the center of a rather large colony, and a place that might otherwise have been bleak and lonely became quite cheerful.

As this was before the time of automobiles, at least practical ones for mountain climbing, and as our house was difficult of access, friends who really wanted to see us were the only ones with the courage to make the trip. And even the valorous ones often nearly succumbed to the difficulties of ascent. I remember our waiting and waiting until we were in despair for the arrival of the Count of Turin for lunch, only to have him and his perspiring aide-de-camp, Count Thaon de Revel, arrive at the foot of the lawn just as we had given up all hope, and ask us if we could send down a couple of our great white oxen to drag up their car, which had broken down halfway up our mountain.

Upon our return to Paris after that year and a half in Vallombrosa, I was amazed one afternoon to have the card of James Gordon Bennett brought in to me. I read his name unbelievingly, as it was a matter of common talk that he did not like me—although no one knew why, least of all myself—and had given the *New York Herald* emphatic instructions to dismiss any operatic success of mine with a bare mention, and not to print my name if it could be helped.

Of course I said I would receive him, and the first thing he remarked when he came into the room was, "Mrs. Story, I have come to make you my deepest apology," and then went on to explain.

It seems that seven years before, in 1893, the same singer who had prevented my Brussels début and alienated Marchesi, had been chagrined at her reception in New York and had cabled to Paris to Mr. Bennett to the effect that the success that was due her had been forestalled by a cable got up by Emma Eames. Mr. Bennett told me that when he received her cable telling of this alleged action of mine he had thought that he had never heard of anything more contemptible, and had immediately cabled the instructions above mentioned to the *Herald*. He went on to say that he had just learned by the merest chance, and from a person who neither knew me nor was particularly interested in me, that this singer had deliberately lied, and therefore he had come that afternoon to "place the *Herald* at my feet." I could have told him that I could not see that its attitude had materially hindered my career, but refrained from doing so.

Bennett in appearance was a hard, austere man and entirely unapproachable. One of the *Herald* men told me later that the reporters had known the facts of this singer's cable all along, but none of them dared to go to Bennett about it. Nevertheless, he possessed a keen sense of justice, as the foregoing proves, and a very tender heart. He adored animals, and perpetuated his affection for them in a motley array of china and painted iron figures of every size which took up a large part of his lawn at Beaulieu. Every time he went to Nice he added to this collection by purchasing a new specimen from a poor old woman who sold such wares.

The spring following his amazing interview with me, he commissioned Julian to paint his portrait, and invited us to visit him at his villa in Beaulieu. While we were there he told us rather a revealing anecdote concerning my dear enemy and colleague. She had the habit, so he said, of always doing something to put him in her debt, usually seating herself at his piano and entertaining his guests by an impromptu song recital after a luncheon or dinner, and immediately afterwards asking some favor of him which he often found difficult to grant and impossible to refuse. At last, one day when he received word from her that she was coming up from Nice to lunch with him, he sent the piano out of the house to forestall her generosity. When she arrived and found it gone, she was perfectly nonplused and asked anxiously what had become of it. All Bennett told her was that it had been sent away for repairs as it was out of order.

The following spring, that of 1901, I sang my last and most successful season in London. I was allowed to sing "Aïda"—probably because it was looked upon as a most unlucky opera!—and made the great impression of my British career in it.

In the seasons that followed I was always offered an engagement at Covent Garden, but as these offers invariably included only the minor rôles of my repertoire—those that I had sung in America merely to accommodate Mr. Grau—and never mentioned "Aïda" after my sensational success in it, or any of my other big rôles, I never considered them. Afterwards I learned that the only reason that I had received even these offers was because King Edward commanded the directors of the opera to engage me each season; and while they complied with the letter of his command, they were careful to couch their offer in such terms as I could not accept and retain my self-respect. In addition, the fee they offered me was much less than that which I received in New York; and as the years went on I found I did not care to add the fatigue of a London season to that of the one in New York. To go to one of our two homes, either in Paris or Vallombrosa, immediately after the American season, and rest, was all I wanted to do. In the end the London proposals became so absurd that I did not bother even to answer them.

After the season that was to be my last in London Mr. Grau came to me and arranged for my next year in America, and again asked me to choose a new rôle; and I told him that I was fired with a desire to sing "Tosca"; that I had heard the great Ternina in the rôle of the jealous prima donna and could not wait to feel the melting phrases of that elemental, emotional heroine in my throat.

He threw up his hands in despair, and exclaimed: "But why choose another failure?"

And I reminded him, "But 'Aïda' did not fail."

He replied, "I know—but 'Tosca'! An opera with a torture scene, a murder, a shooting and a suicide! Not even you could make the public like it."

But I insisted, and in the end he capitulated and consented to my singing it.

VI

AFTER Mr. Grau agreed to my singing "Tosca" at the Metropolitan, I abandoned myself to the study of the rôle and became so absorbed that I could hardly eat or sleep. I had seen Sarah Bernhardt's first performance as Sardou's famous heroine in Paris, and the thrill of that night remained with me after all those years. She had gripped her audience even when her back was turned. And that is an accomplishment not to be lightly scorned. It proves that one has risen above mere gesture and expression and is holding one's audience with the power of thought. Although one is unconscious of the strain at the time of the performance, there is none greater than keeping in character during the three or four hours necessary to the presentation of the average opera. And the wise artist rejoices over any moment of respite wherein she may conserve her vitality and strength for emotional scenes.

In the beginning of my career, before I had known sickness or trouble, I not only felt no need for such fleeting moments of relaxation, but I did not realize that they were necessary to any well balanced or profound portrayal. Perhaps this was because when one is young, one is incapable of reaching the heights in interpretation. But, as the years went on, and I found each performance exhausting me more and more until at last I was compelled to spend the day succeeding each in a darkened room with my poor, overtaxed heart beating a million to the minute, I came to appreciate thoroughly Bernhardt's wisdom in occasionally turning her back to her audience in order to relax the tension. And taking a lesson out of her great unwritten book of the technic of acting, I did likewise.

As an additional act of self-preservation, I had a clause inserted in my contract to the effect that I should be called upon for only so many performances a month, and that two full calendar days should elapse between the dates of my performances. This allowed me what I have always called one day of death after each performance. It was absolutely necessary. If I denied my nerves these twenty-four hours of rest, as I was persuaded to do once or twice, I invariably paid by losing a performance later in the month. It is pertinent to note that it was Mr. Grau and not myself who suggested and evolved that life-saving clause. Incidentally, it later caused the Gatti-Casazza régime a great deal of anguish.

"Tosca" duplicated the sensation made by the revival of "Aïda," and it does not need to be pointed out to the thousands of opera goers who witness my dozens of successors in that now familiar rôle that the opera has become a mainstay of repertoire. The audiences at each performance seemed fairly hypnotized by its tragic story and impassioned music; and one memorable evening in Philadelphia, when after the tense stillness of suspense I at last gave the *coup de grâce* to Scarpia, a veritable roar of relief rose from the packed auditorium. In spite of my emotional portrayal of "Aïda" few believed I had it in me to give a convincing one of so emotional a rôle as that of Tosca. Because I had sung restrained rôles with restraint and had never mistaken mere explosiveness for drama, my potential passion was not suspected.

One night, during the same scene, the tablecloth caught fire from one of the candles. As nothing ever startled me on the stage, I did not come out of character for even a second, but dipped a napkin in a finger bowl, put the

As Tosca

fire out and continued as though nothing had happened. The act was purely mechanical, and unattended by fear or excitement. One is in such a state of exaltation on the stage that there is no room in one's consciousness for the ordinary emotions or panics.

The year of the "Tosca" success, which was the last of the management of that great director and artist, Maurice Grau, I also promised to sing in a revival of "Ero e Leandro," in the "Ballo in Maschera," and the rôle of Fiordiligi in "Cosi Fan Tutte."

That summer I studied "Cosi Fan Tutte" with an accompanist in my country home. And although neither he nor I had ever heard the opera, it is interesting to note that when we went to Munich to hear a performance of "Cosi Fan Tutte" at the Regent's Theater there, we found that instinctively we had given the opera the correct tradition and *tempi* throughout, with the exception of one concerted number at the end.

The "Ballo in Maschera" presented a peculiar problem to me. Being much younger than the majority of my contemporaries, I had not been trained in the tradition of the early Italian school, the essence of which is a certain superficiality, and which is necessary to the interpretation of this opera. This school prohibited gesture and singing simultaneously. But I found that in such operas as the "Ballo in Maschera" and "Trovatore," which I sang later with Caruso, any deeply emotional note or attempted earnestness of feeling was a waste of energy, and even destroyed the color necessary to their correct interpretation. One had to keep on a note of theatrical artificiality and count upon accent and phrasing to give an impression of emotion. In other words, I had to learn to sing them objectively instead of subjectively as I did other operas. Had I used the same method of self-hypnotism and self-effacement in portraying these rôles that I brought to my other interpretations, I would have exhausted myself and have been less effective.

Various portraits in the Brera Gallery, in Milan, were the inspiration for my costumes for the "Ballo in Maschera." The Carpaccio paintings in Venice inspired my Desdemona costumes; and those who saw the headdress in the third act have easily recognized the famous Beatrice d'Este head, with which every school-child is familiar.

Inspired by the unusual beauty of the costumes Doucet had made for Sybil Sanderson's Manon, I went to this couturier for the costumes for "Cosi Fan Tutte." They, as well as my coiffures, were copied to the last detail from portraits of the Princesses, Adelaide and Louise, by Nattier, at Versailles. Afterwards I wore them in the "Nozze di Figaro" under the leadership of Mahler.

It was always my custom, whenever confronted with the dressing of a new rôle, to buy photographs of the various paintings I considered most representative of the period of the opera and give them to my couturier to be used as models. Undoubtedly this practice, combined with the startling success of my costumes, was the reason that Julian was always credited with designing them. While I have no doubt that my husband would have been more than capable of doing so, the fact remains that not only did he never make any suggestions concerning my stage dresses, but he never saw one of them until it was finished.

The "Ballo in Maschera," the "Faust," the "Trovatore," the Doña Anna—in "Don Giovanni"—and the first "Nozze di Figaro" costumes were made for me by Worth. The "Aïda," Desdemona and first "Tosca" costumes were the work of a woman of very great genius, who, although extremely young at the time I knew her, was nevertheless the head of a large firm of costumiers in Paris, Madame Landolf by name. The blue cloak and blue muslin veil I used in "Aïda" were my own invention, born of my desire to be hardly visible when I first appeared, to seem to melt into the moonlight of the third act. Worth made my second set of "Tosca" costumes after the first had been destroyed in the San Francisco earthquake and fire.

When I had several new rôles to sing, as I did have that season of the "Tosca" revival, I always made it a point to give the different sets of costumes to different dressmakers, as I realized that they could not be equally interested in all, and therefore preferred to have each one concentrate on one type of gown.

At the beginning of this season of 1902-03, Julian's physician told me that my husband's only hope of keeping well lay in work, activity and plenty of occupation for his brain. Therefore he was installed in a studio in Philadelphia where he had many friends, and from whence he came to New York frequently to see me and to hear me sing.

This winter I had again counted too much on my vitality and strength, and after two or three appearances, which included my success in "Tosca," I had another breakdown which again robbed me of my voice, as had the first, which it much resembled, with a few little additions such as a very subnormal temperature, neuritis and nodules on my vocal cords. The latter were singer's nodules such as are sometimes caused by singing with relaxed or red cords, and are easily cured by complete silence. I was again ordered an eighteen months' rest and banished from New York at once; but not wishing to sail without my husband, I went to Newport to remain until he had completed his work.

I am really ashamed to write of all these breakdowns, because it makes me appear a sort of Job; but as I never allowed myself the luxury of self-pity or brooding over my misfortune and only lived in anticipation of the time that I should be able to sing again, they never affected my work or my spirit. As each moment passed, I put it behind me, realizing that dwelling upon painful things impresses them more indelibly on one's mind and weakens one for the future.

We sailed direct to Italy that summer, and I had my first view of the Bay of Naples, a wonderful approach to that divinely beautiful country.

As I seem to be deserting the land of my

citizenship continually in this record, it might be well to explain that circumstance turned me, as stanch an American as could be found, into a resident of Europe. In the first place, the climate of America proved to be too stimulating for one of my temperament and highly strung nerves. It kept me in such a state of tension that I was rarely able to sing two successive seasons at the Metropolitan until after 1904 and 1905. And even in the years I could sing, I was twice unable to undertake the supplementary tour the opera company made every season. It was only by detaching myself completely from the life about me that it was possible for me to keep myself in a reasonable state of calm while there. Other reasons were that Julian had been educated at Eton and Oxford, in England, had never been to America until he went there with me, owned property in Paris and subsequently at Vallombrosa, and that all his friends, as well as a great many of mine, were in Europe. Therefore, after I came to Paris to study in 1886, I never really lived in America again with the exception of a short period during the War.

The next winter Julian returned to Philadelphia to work, and I remained in Paris. This was the first year of Conried's régime, in which he declared himself determined "to get along without stars," including myself, a decision for which I was most grateful that year because of my health.

Shortly after my return to Paris to recuperate in 1903, James Gordon Bennett sent me word by his private secretary that a rumor was being circulated by the singer "who still pursued me" to the effect that I was paralyzed and would never sing again. Mr. Bennett pointed out that it was impossible for me to deny this, as no one ever believed a denial under any circumstances. He also said that any answer I made to this rumor would only call attention to it, even as a denial of any statement in the public press only served to call the attention of the thousands who had not read the original article to the item. He followed his secretary's visit with a personal call, and the demand that I do something to bring myself before the public, saying that he would see to it that the news thereof was cabled in full to the *Herald*.

I asked: "But what can I do? I am far from well, although I am equally far from being paralyzed, and had planned to do nothing this year."

Then he declared; "You can give some parties."

Some Memories and Reflections

I felt as much like giving a party as I did like climbing a steeple, but nevertheless I did give four musicales in the studio of our house at 7 Place des Etats-Unis on four consecutive Thursdays—always my favorite day for receiving. They were the most brilliant of any for which I was ever responsible. The studio, opening as it did into the dining room and conservatory, made an ideal place in which to receive, and had, as well, perfect acoustic properties. It measured ten meters by ten, or nearly thirty-three feet square, with a very lofty ceiling. At each party I sang, and, as was always the case when I was confronted with the necessity of singing, I was at my best in spite of my health. After each one, Bennett had a lengthy article, including a list of the brilliant company and the names of the famous musicians who took part in the program, cabled to the *Herald* in New York.

One of my friends, knowing that I never made use of the newspapers, was perfectly amazed at this overwhelming burst of publicity, and to this day has never ceased to speak of that particular paper as "your *New York Herald.*"

At the close of the winter in Paris I went to

Italy for the summer. Upon my return, Mr. Carré of the Opéra Comique, asked me to take part in a benefit performance for the artists' home at Pont-aux-Dames. The receipts from this performance were to be used to establish a bed for the singers of the Opéra Comique. Feeling that to appear in Paris only in concert after an absence of so many years would be fair neither to myself nor to my reputation, I told Mr. Carré that I would rather give a performance of "Tosca," always provided it could be sung in Italian. He seemed delighted with the idea and begged that I communicate with the others of the Metropolitan cast who, by lucky chance, happened to be actually singing at Drury Lane that autumn under the direction of Campanini. I got in touch with them at once, and the result was that in my operatic reappearance in Paris I was supported by Scotti, the greatest Scarpia America has ever known, and de Marchi as Mario, with Campanini conducting.

I had been seeing Sarah Bernhardt frequently that year, and when I told her of the proposed "Tosca" she was enormously interested and, saying that she must put me in immediate touch with Sardou, she telephoned him and told him of the imminent performance, and arranged for him to lunch with her at my house three days later.

The day of the luncheon, Bernhardt's unique little carriage, which, although built like a hansom, had four wheels, pulled up at my door, and Sarah stepped out clad in a white cloth dress, trimmed with white fur and elaborately embroidered, after the mode of the time, and crowned with a wreath of pink roses in lieu of a hat. I had duplicated the seating arrangement used in her own home—a throne-like chair with its back to the light, at the head of the table—and she was delightfully surprised at the attention and most appreciative. Sardou, upon his arrival, proved to be charming and, although he was not to live many years afterwards, as gay and irresponsible as a boy. My inseparable friend, Miss Fetridge, was our only other guest, and after luncheon the five of us spent a long afternoon of stimulating and amusing talk.

Among other things Sarah begged me never to come to see her play without letting her know in advance. I, fearing to be indiscreet, protested that she could never bother with seeing me each time I attended one of her performances.

"Oh, I didn't mean that," she replied, "I

meant that I wanted to know when you were going to be in the audience so I would be sure really to *act* that night."

She was a commercialized genius. I attended the première of both her "Tosca" and her "Cleopatra," and the impression they made was overwhelming. How little I dreamed at that first "Tosca" performance that I should ever be playing the rôle!

Puccini came from Italy in order to be present at the "Tosca" performance, and both he and Sardou attended the rehearsals. During one rehearsal, Puccini suggested that I hold each of the last high notes at the end of the famous *Vissi d'arte* aria as long as I possibly could. I told him that, to my mind, to hold three notes as long as possible and at the top of my voice seemed more like shouting than singing, and that, as it was my custom always to make but *one* climax and *only one,* he could choose which of the three notes he wished me to hold. He was much amused and, having faith in my ability, gave me my head. I was told afterwards that he considered my Tosca unique, quite different from any other he had ever heard sung and possessing the deep note of Greek tragedy.

Sardou's suggestion at rehearsals was one

233

of which all ambitious Scarpias should take note—namely, that in the great scene before Tosca stabs him, Scarpia should never *touch* her, but instead hover over her wholly evil, almost vulture-like. He also showed me how to stab Scarpia with the most dramatic effect and get away from him before he fell. Apropos of getting out of Scarpia's way, I shall never forget my first New York performance of "Tosca." I had stabbed Scarpia and, not calculating for my train in getting away from him, I had made my wild rush away backstage with him lying with his full weight in the middle of it. I fell flat, of course, and knocked the chair behind him over in the bargain. I hit the floor with such a violence that my leg was fearfully bruised, but I was so excited at the time of the accident that I noticed no pain. I was afterwards told that the public thought the fall was taken intentionally and was considered a wonderful bit of "business." Certainly it was not one I cared to repeat.

Afterwards, in order to avoid a repetition of this incident, I always walked across the stage a little beyond where I must ultimately stand to kill him and then *turned* and walked back, thus leaving my train on the side farthest from him. I was then correctly placed to

Photograph by Aimé Dupont

As Tosca

pick up the knife with my right hand, thrust it into Scarpia's breast with a twist of my body, and then make my dash to the back of the stage without danger of being tripped.

In those days opera had not become a craze, like a much-advertised breakfast food of which every one is supposed to partake in order to belong to the enlightened, as it is to-day. Then people would not come to an opera which did not have some particular quality of appeal of merit and that was not well cast. As I have said before, operas like "Aïda" and "Tosca," that have since become the mainstays of the repertoire, had no drawing power whatsoever.

It was a period, instead, of romance and poetry and idealism, and even those not romantic, idealistic or poetic followed the general trend. Therefore I was extremely fortunate, in the light of my particular gifts which best fitted me for youthful, romantic rôles, in coming at such a time. And not the least of my good fortune was in having such a director as Maurice Grau.

Mr. Grau always said that he knew little about music and very little about singing, but that he could always pick the artist who had the spark. He not only had this invariable instinct for what I call quality, but he also seemed to know intuitively how to get the best out of each singer. I remember his saying of one artist of our company—a genius, but most eccentric—that he had to give her her head in order that she might be able to sing at all. And it was with this same tact and understanding that he treated all of us. He realized that one could not have quality and still be able to turn on one's voice like a talking machine. I never knew him really to complain when a performance was canceled because of some artist's inability to appear. The only thing he wanted was that we should communicate to the public the emotions we had given it a right to expect of us, and he knew that in order to do that we had to be fresh and feeling at our best.

He had a passion for order, and order is heaven's first law. He had a large tablet on which was planned for four to six weeks ahead all the operas to be given, with their casts, and alternate casts in case one or more of his artists should fall ill. He arranged all rehearsals with the same marvelous sense of system, and this methodical management enabled his singers to order their days in quiet and peace. They knew, under his régime, the periods that were theirs for rest and the days for work; and those who wished to give quality to their work instead of permitting it to degenerate into meaningless sound and movement were given opportunity to conjure up the mood and enthusiasm absolutely necessary for such interpretations.

As many rehearsals were impossible at the Metropolitan, Mr. Grau did not consider it any place for beginners and therefore chose his artists—usually Europeans from necessity—from those who had won their spurs, who had what they call *acquis* in France, or experience in the theater. I was considered the great exception to this rule, but nevertheless I had had experience in concert and two full years of opera before he engaged me.

I have often heard him discuss singers, even experienced singers, who later were to thrill America, and he could almost always prophesy to the month how soon they could hope to appeal to and hold the discriminating American public. He would say: "In two years he (or she) will be ripe to appear in America."

He made amazingly few mistakes, and those he made were invariably about singers thrust upon him and not about those he chose himself.

He was extremely just, but withal appallingly keen in business matters. If a singer had carelessly permitted a clause to be inserted

237

in his contract that might be construed to his disadvantage, Mr. Grau was quite capable of so construing it; and it was incumbent upon that singer to eliminate or modify such a clause when he came to make his next contract. Jean de Reszke used to say that while Mr. Grau had no mean streak in him, he always looked out for himself and enforced the exact letter of his agreement. Jean said: "Maurice will give you a cigar, but he would refuse to give you a match to light it with, if it wasn't in the bargain." But whenever Mr. Grau felt that an artist should have some privilege or advantage that it was inadvisable to name in the contract and gave his word to the artist thereto, that singer could always depend upon it that Mr. Grau's word would prove better than his signature.

No one who knew the man ever had reason for a moment to doubt his absolute probity. But for all his integrity of character and spirit and his fine simplicity, he was capable of being exceedingly rough at times. There was, for example, a certain German singer whose husband was always moving about among the standees and telling them how much better his wife could sing the same rôle than the prima donna appearing that evening.

One day this woman became very angry and made a scene with Grau over being paid a lower fee than she considered she was worth. He answered her tirade brutally: "Singers who draw big houses are worth big money. I can't understand why you think you're one of them. No one has ever demanded his money back because a performance of yours was canceled."

He then proceeded to add insult to injury by forbidding her husband the opera house even when she sang, refusing him all complimentary tickets; and ultimately the husband was obliged to subscribe to a box in order to attend the performance of any opera.

He banned all backstage gossip and believed that aloofness on the part of his artists increased the public's interest in them. He declared that the public was entitled only to what it paid for, and that intimate details of the lives of the singers—some of them adding neither savor nor dignity to the company—were not part of the bargain. He was relentless in tracing a leak and dismissing its perpetrator.

He had little difficulty with me in this regard. Quite the contrary. In fact, one anonymous letter-writer—this was the day before the phrase of the "poison pen" was used—was so incensed by my aloofness that she (or he) sat down and wrote me a long and most exasperated screed, in which he (or she) raved violently about my "holier than thou" expression. I must say that I never dreamed that I had any such expression. Having had it instilled into me by my grandmother that an unattainable state of perfection was the normal standard of humanity, and always being humiliated by the realization that no matter how "good" I might be I always fell short of what I believed was the average virtue, I never was self-righteous. Coming in contact with so few people, I took it for granted, not being critical or suspicious, that others had attained the high ideal of conduct toward which I was striving.

Mr. Grau was never at a loss for a retort. As Edouard de Reszke had first call on the rôles which he and Pol Plançon sang in common, it so happened that it was necessary for Mr. Grau to send Pol Plançon hither and yon to fill various concert engagements in order to make use of the number of performances for which Plançon was engaged. Plançon strongly objected to this "being sent around the country like a trunk," as he expressed it, and often engaged Grau in violent argument about it. One day one of these discussions grew so acrid that Mr. Plançon ended by calling Mr. Grau "a dirty Jew."

Whereupon Mr. Grau answered quickly: "A Jew, yes—and I wish I were a better one. But dirty, no."

During the winter 1903-04 Mr. Grau performed the last of his many kindnesses to me by making a contract for me with the Wolfsohn Bureau for a continent-wide concert tour of America, which, it was agreed, I was to undertake in the autumn of 1905 just prior to the Metropolitan season.

In the summer of 1904 Mr. Conried came to see me, and I found him most amusing and natural and totally without affectation or pose. He told me that he had tried to abolish stars, myself among the first, but that the public would not permit him to do so and had besieged him with letters demanding my reëngagement and would I sign again at the Metropolitan the next season? I agreed to do so—at a greatly augmented fee!

Mr. Conried followed scrupulously in the footsteps of Mr. Grau in so far as perfect order in the organization of the company and performances were concerned. And it was undoubtedly to his so doing that he owed the continued great success of his venture. In addition he attached a great deal of importance to scenery and stage mechanism, and this he greatly improved at the Metropolitan.

However, the Metropolitan Opera House, both before and after the fire, always had extremely good acoustic properties. But, unlike those at Covent Garden, where anybody can be heard, they demanded concentration of tone. With the least spreading or forcing of the voice it became inaudible. I shall never forget the ignominious failure of an excellent singer to whom I had explained these acoustic peculiarities of the opera house I knew so well. I had warned her that she must be careful about forcing and, above all, not to shout, and some kind friend to whom she related my warning said: "Pooh, it isn't so. Let out your voice as much as you please. Emma Eames just told you that because she wanted you to fail." She accepted the advice of her scatter-brained friend instead of that of the experienced singer, and her season at the Metropolitan was both brief and humiliating.

To the voice that is concentrated and controlled, there is no more grateful place in which to sing. Of course, the effects must be broad. Details and subtle shades, such as are possible to "opéra comique," as it is called in

France, are completely absorbed by the vastness of the auditorium.

Another charm of the Metropolitan is its dressing rooms. They have clean painted walls, simple furnishings and every possible convenience. Only a singer who has dressed in the dog kennels assigned to the artists at Covent Garden and in the bare rooms at the opera houses on tour can thoroughly appreciate them. At Covent Garden, where the auditorium is beautiful in its simplicity and graceful tiers of boxes that mount to the top, the dressing rooms were never really clean, were below the level of a side street on which was the famous market of the same name and were permeated by the odor of decaying vegetables. And if the opera to be sung called for more than one star, they were divided off by movable partitions into even smaller compartments. An enterprising organ grinder usually stationed himself and his instrument just outside our windows, while we were dressing, where he proceeded to grind out hackneyed tunes until he was well paid to take himself off. It was in one of these gorgeous apartments that I received the Prince of Wales between the acts every night that I sang in London!

243

SOME MEMORIES AND REFLECTIONS

At the Paris Opéra, which was as vast as a city, each principal singer was given an unfurnished room with a small dressing room attached. In the latter there was the most primitive sort of a closet in which might be placed a washstand and other toilet accessories. There was no plumbing whatsoever. The furniture and hangings used in the outer room, with the exception of two small chairs and a table, had to be supplied by the singer then in possession, and usually were indicative of the state of his finances as well as his taste.

I have often been asked, in connection with the Paris Opéra, to substantiate the popular belief that the path of a young and good-looking singer is beset with pitfalls, by relating any painful experiences that were mine there. Either my utter ignorance of life and inability to suspect evil built up an impenetrable wall about me, or else the operatic overlords with whom I came in contact in Paris were unusually circumspect; but the truth is that, during the two years I was engaged at the Opéra, I never had one word spoken to me to which any exception could be taken.

The contract which I signed with Mr. Conried for the season of 1904-05 at the Metro-

politan was the same as the one I had always
made with Maurice Grau, and specified all the
principal rôles of my repertoire with the one
exception of Eva in "The Meistersinger."
Grau had persuaded me to learn this last
opera in German, and sing it with German
singers, and under a very secondary German
conductor, now dead and happily beyond all
condemnation. Not even the Kaiser himself
could have been more autocratic than this director. He attached more value to the words
than to the music and declared the hold at the
end of the quintette, which gives such an effect
of breadth and exaltation to that beautiful
number, to be absolutely taboo, although Seidl,
who was Wagner's pupil, allowed it. Having
sung the opera with artists who knew how to
sing and did not bark in the traditional German fashion, and with a leader who understood his business, I told Mr. Grau after the
first disheartening performance that I did not
feel that I could appear in the two remaining
performances of the three I had agreed upon.
As usual, he understood perfectly and did not
insist. Therefore, the next evening "The
Meistersinger" was given, the singer who had
the rôle of the father, and who had spent his
entire time during the first presentation telling

me how much better he sang Hans Sachs than the man to whom the part had been assigned, had to pour his grievances into another and, I hope, more sympathetic ear.

After that experience, I never again included Eva in my repertoire and, as though aware of my dislike of the rôle, the Covent Garden directors invariably offered it with two or three others which did not appeal to me, as bait for the London season!

Upon my return to America in the fall of 1904, I found that my rest had done me an enormous amount of good, and that I had not only gained strength, but a knowledge and possession of myself that I had never had before.

That winter, having found hotel life very tiring, entailing as it did constant contact with crowds of people—I could not enter or leave my suite without encountering them—I took furnished apartments on Fifty-eighth Street. And it was from there that I attended the Kreisler and Ysaye concert, which always was to remain one of the most beautiful impressions of my life. Their playing of the concerto by Bach for two violins was so inspired that tears of joy poured down my face. Such moments are a foretaste of heaven.

As Eva in "Die Meistersinger"

The summer following I went directly to Italy without stopping in Paris, as I was obliged to be back in America much earlier than was my custom on account of the concert tour under Wolfsohn which was to begin with the great Maine festival in September.

This concert tour proved to be delightful from beginning to end. I had engaged a private car in defiance of all my friends, who told me that a private car was always out of order, was always attached to the worst trains and was always late, that the service thereon was wretched and that it was all very well to boast of its bathroom, but wait until I tried to get a bath in it! But, as is usually the case when the worst is predicted, the weeks I lived in my traveling home were an unalloyed delight. Our railways in America are so wonderfully equipped, so perfectly organized and the rails so smoothly laid that one hardly realizes one is not in a hotel. My car was furnished with beds, not berths, and as it was made to accommodate a number of people, Miss Fetridge, my maid and I, who were its sole occupants en tour, had any amount of room.

Sharing the program with me on this tour were Emilio de Gogorza and Mr. Holman, cellist. Mr. Webber, an old friend of mine, and one with whom both the de Reszkes and I had prepared our Wagnerian rôles, was our accompanist.

Mr. de Gogorza had an immediate and immense success, which, unversed as I was in the proper traditions governing a prima donna and her "support," he was allowed by me to enjoy. I have heard since that a "support" of any kind is not allowed to have all the success he inspires and his recalls are cut down to a very limited number, no matter what the enthusiasm of the audience may be.

When I had first heard him sing at Miss Callendar's prior to the tour, I had been afraid that his voice was too small to blend well with mine in our duets, and was only too delighted to discover that I had erred in my judgment. Mr. Wolfsohn had had some difficulty in persuading him to come with us, as Mr. de Gogorza had more or less decided to give up the concert stage at the time. All this must seem most amusing to those who have had the joy of hearing him all these years.

Holman was excellently received, too, but as he was invariably referred to as the "venerable Dutch cellist," although hardly fifty, he was furiously angry most of the trip. Another thing that added to his indignation was the fact that, in the small towns, there were no porters at the stations to carry his bags and his precious cello which he called "Mrs. Holman." I shall never forget his explosion over this omission upon our arrival in each little place, and his terrible threat that he intended to write a letter to the *Figaro*—in Paris, mind you!—about it.

Melville Stone, then manager of the Associated Press and a valued personal friend of mine, gave me letters to various people throughout the country, and I was royally entertained and taken on innumerable personally conducted tours through the various cities of our itinerary, thus receiving a liberal education in their topography and existing social conditions.

The tour lasted nine weeks, beginning on the thirteenth of October—again the fatal number thirteen—and ending on the thirteenth of December in Providence. I boarded my car at Toronto, and journeyed as far north and west as beautiful Vancouver and Victoria, through a country still to a great extent clothed in virgin forest. It was a trip of unforgettable beauty. We went by water from Vancouver to Victoria, and back through a narrow channel bounded on either hand by low-lying wooded hills. In my remembrances of that country, Stanley Park at Vancouver stands out as something particularly lovely. It was the gift of a patriotic nature-loving citizen and consisted of a large tract of virgin forest. One of the conditions of the gift was that none of the trees were to be cut down except in the making of the necessary roads. This condition has been respected and the trees left untouched to grow in their own sweet way. Giant trees may be seen growing out of the flanks of others equally gigantic that have lain undisturbed where they have fallen.

During this trip we also visited other cities of the northwest, among them Spokane, Tacoma, Portland, Oregon, and Seattle on the beautiful Puget Sound. Thence we traveled south to San Francisco.

In the last-named city Miss Fetridge and I were again entertained by Dr. Tevis, who had newly rebuilt his delightful house on what was familiarly called Nob Hill; and it was agreed that when we returned with the Opera Company in the following spring, we were to go directly to his home and remain there as his guests during our sojourn in San Francisco.

We returned by way of the Arizona desert,

which we found still beautiful and undulating in outline, but wearing the gray pallor of death that it takes on during the arid months of summer and autumn. Seeing it so, it did not seem possible that any amount of irrigation ever could make that dreary waste bloom. And yet, upon my return to California with the Opera Company in the spring, when I raised the curtain beside my berth after our first night in the desert—I am always most eager to see daylight after a night on the train—expecting to see the same gray, cheerless scene I had witnessed the previous December, I was amazed to behold the most gorgeous flower garden conceivable. No planted garden could have been more luxuriant. The cacti were covered with blooms of indescribable beauty and color, and every apparently dead shrub had blossomed.

After the concert tour I returned to New York, as I have said before, and sang in "Trovatore" with Caruso for the first time. Caruso was one of Conried's innovations, as Mr. Grau had never seemed to be able to come to an understanding with the great tenor. The first of April the entire company was taken to San Francisco for the annual season there, and it was decided that my first performance in that city was to be with Sembrich in the "Nozze di Figaro" on the sixth of April.

Upon our arrival Miss Fetridge and I went at once to Nob Hill, as we had promised Dr. Tevis the preceding autumn, and a party was arranged for the evening of the same day on which my first performance in matinée was to take place. For this party I was to sing, and Madame Sembrich had planned with me the surprise of singing the letter duet from the "Nozze" to end the program, in addition to the numbers I was to contribute.

Dr. Tevis had received a letter from a friend asking him to invite a certain person to the party to whom he did not wish to send an invitation. After long and anxious deliberation, he tossed this letter in the air with the remark: "This letter will answer itself!" He little thought by what a cataclysm it would be answered.

I was given a lovely room opening out on to a charming balcony, built in the Italian style with a fountain at one end and an entrance to the drawing-room at the other. An enormous window formed one end of the latter and overlooked the town and the bay, with Oakland in the distance.

On the night of April the fifth, with no

thought of the morrow, I retired to my room and its immense four-poster of solid mahogany, overhung with the heavy wooden canopy usual to such beds.

VII

ARLY the next morning—afterwards I learned it was about five o'clock—the world set up a tremendous roaring and rocking. The house rolled and pitched as though it were in a heavy sea. The great earthquake had begun.

To be taken by Mother Nature and shaken as a terrier would a rat makes one feel very unimportant. It was this feeling of insignificance, I suppose, that made one take so little thought for the saving of oneself or one's personal effects.

The pitching developed into more and more abrupt jerks until the great bed, a heavy mahogany four-poster in which I was lying, was gradually shaken from the wall out into the center of the room.

I realized that we were in the throes of an earthquake. Objects were falling all about me, and not wishing to see them, I buried my face, and clung with both hands to the bed in order not to be thrown out, and waited for the shocks to cease. I remained in bed because I did not wish to risk being maimed by the crashing

254

glass and the things that were being hurled about the room at each shock. I knew that if the heavy canopy of the bed which was swaying above me, fell, it would kill me outright, and that I much preferred to being crippled.

I was conscious of the rattling of the bed and of the rumbling, roaring sound of the earthquake like the roaring of thunder. Vases fell in my room and two electric lamps, but I did not hear them fall; all other sounds were drowned in the noise of the earthquake itself. On the terrace outside my window were large urns filled with flowers, and screwed on to the balustrade. These urns were wrenched off by the shaking and thrown down on to the floor of the terrace. The great chimney of a powerhouse on an adjoining lot crashed to the ground.

The duration of this quake has been estimated as a certain number of seconds, but it seemed to me hours before it was quiet enough for me to dare to open my eyes. And while I have always believed that perhaps the first tremor could be calculated in seconds, the succession of shocks which followed must have lasted minutes, not seconds.

At last the earthquake subsided except for

an occasional little tremor as a reminder, and I was beginning to think about getting up when our host knocked at my door.

At first, still dazed from the shaking, I did not answer. Then realizing that he wished to speak to me, I flung on a dressing-gown and opened the door, to have him greet me with: "Don't be afraid! Don't be afraid! Don't be afraid! It's all over!"

I answered: "I'm not afraid."

He stared at me a second and asked:

"Do you know what it actually was?"

Quite coolly, I said: "I suppose it was an earthquake," being conscious of no sense of fear.

He laughed and commented: "Well, I'm glad you're enjoying it. Let's go and see what Fanny is doing."

We then went to the rooms of Miss Fetridge and my maid. We found the former calmly shaking pieces of glass out of her slippers. My maid, a Frenchwoman on her first visit to this country, was perfectly unmoved. She had already had so many surprises that she probably imagined it was only one more of the natural phenomena. She told us, though, that when she saw a man running through the street in his nightshirt, bareheaded and shrieking, she thought something unusual must be happening. Then she went back to bed and to sleep. As I was to sing the rôle of the Countess in the "Nozze di Figaro" that afternoon, my first thought was whether a performance would take place under the circumstances. My host said that no one would dare to go into a theater after such a terrible earthquake shock for fear of the building collapsing. I tried to telephone to our manager, but of course the wires were down. Then I realized that there could be no performance. We then walked about the house to see what damage had been done. We found that the house itself had suffered little, but the ruins of valuable vases, china and glass strewed the floor.

I felt an immense exhilaration, a need to be *doing* something.

On coming upstairs again, we stepped out on to the terrace of my room, and there a peaceful, delicious morning breeze met us, and the song of birds.

The moon in her last quarter was near the horizon, and suddenly we saw one little tongue of flame in the distance. It was very far away, down by the Oakland Ferry, and as the air was so still we apprehended nothing from that source.

257

I then dressed myself, for I thought I would go down to the Hotel St. Francis and try and find Madame Sembrich who was staying there. It had occurred to us that she would be less well off on the sixth story of a modern skyscraper than we were in a house built to resist the light earthquake shocks which are of frequent occurrence in California—and in this case it proved it could resist a pretty severe one. On emerging from the house, we were fortunate enough to find an acquaintance passing in an automobile, who happened to be going our way. He agreed to take us to the Hotel St. Francis and call for us on his way back.

On our arrival at the hotel we found people in every stage of undress and in little quiet groups. Restlessness there was, but no noise or hysterics that I saw. All electric communication being stopped, there were little guttering candles placed about where lights were necessary.

In the hotel office we asked for Madame Sembrich and were given a pass to go up to her apartment. It was quite an unnecessary formality, as people were passing up and down as they pleased, and we were unchallenged at any time.

"Nozze di Figaro"
Period Louis xv
1909

Up the six flights of stairs and back we went. Great masses of plaster were down in every direction, and in passing the drawing-room we saw the concert grand piano flung more than halfway across the room. We arrived at Madame Sembrich's apartment and called and pounded in vain, and were just leaving the hotel when it occurred to us that she might be in the dining room. Sure enough, we found here there, she having hurriedly thrown on a few garments and left her apartment as soon as the first quake had subsided.

Having seen the ease with which people entered the hotel, we persuaded her to go up to her room and get her valuables and enough clothing to pass the night, and come up to us on the hill. She gladly consented, saying she would follow us as soon as she could get ready. My host also invited M. Plançon and Mr. Dippel to lunch.

While at the hotel we learned that the theater where the rest of our season of opera was to have taken place was shaken up badly. The roof had fallen in and the balconies had been thrown into the pit.

Shortly after we had returned home and while Madame Sembrich was in her apartment making ready to come to us, we had another short but rather severe shock, and she hurried down to us, bringing only her jewels and a small bag of necessaries. So little provision had she made that, later, I was even obliged to give her one of my own cloaks.

We next learned that the water mains had parted, that San Francisco was at the mercy of the flames, and cut off from all communication with the outside world.

From the big window of the house, we had all of Chinatown and the business portion of San Francisco mapped out before us, down to the wharves and out to Oakland across the bay. It seemed to us merely a spectacle, and not even a particularly thrilling one, as all through the day we watched it.

At frequent intervals there were new shocks, but they could only be considered feeble in comparison with the first. Each time a shock occurred, Madame Sembrich's faithful Frieda went into another room and put on her hat, and when the quake had died down, she took it off again.

At one o'clock we had a small hot meal. It was taken upstairs in the big drawing-room, as we wanted to remain where we could watch the fires. The sight, first of the enormous high office buildings, and then the steeple of a church, lapped in flames, fascinated us. The fire would recede, and then we would conjecture which direction it was going to take next. It never occurred to us that it could climb the hill to us.

In the afternoon the recurring shocks became a bit exasperating, and we went down into the garden and sat there. It began to be very sultry as the fire, though distant, was raging on two sides of the hill and surrounding it, and great flakes of burned material fell on us.

We went out from time to time to the edge of the hill, where the Fairmount Hotel now stands, to watch the progress of the flames, and everywhere camped out about the houses in that neighborhood were groups of Chinese, whole families of them, quite quiet, quite cheerful, and very picturesque. They felt the hill was safe, as we all did. We imagined they could easily prevent the hill being destroyed by dynamiting blocks of houses at the base, as the only wind of any force blew away from us and towards the burning city. The fire did spare the hill, as may be remembered, and went around and beyond it to Van Ness Avenue; then suddenly the wind veered about in the opposite direction and swept the flames over that part of the city that had previously been spared, including the hill we had thought so safe.

In speaking of this double calamity that fell on San Francisco, the Californians have always belittled the part played in it by the earthquake. They refer to it more often as the "great fire."

Towards the middle of the afternoon—one no longer took any account of time—Dr. Tevis, our host, told us the Fire Department had sent word to him that it was dangerous to have a fire in the kitchen, as most chimneys had been cracked by the earthquake, and the house might be set on fire.

I tired, finally, of looking at the "fireworks" and started to play patience, much to the indignation of Plançon, who said I was not "in the picture" at all, that I had no sentiment of the earthquake, and was a "rock." Plançon said the earthquake was a visitation to him for having come out to California with us instead of having gone back to the marriage of his niece. To this Madame Sembrich replied that it was a pity so many had been made to suffer for so small a sin on his part!

As far as I was concerned, after the shake

good old Mother Nature had given us in the morning, nothing seemed to matter, myself least of all. I suppose I was paralyzed and awed by the immensity of it all, for in order to try and realize it I had to say to myself from time to time that there had been an earthquake, and that I was watching the destruction of a city—a great and prosperous one at the zenith of its success. I could not *thrill,* although I could have found strength to *do* anything I might be called upon to do.

We were to have some food brought up: sandwiches, eggs and bouillon, the last two to be warmed or cooked by us. However, we were all much too excited to eat anything, and were contented with a cup of bouillon.

About eight o'clock in the evening Dr. Tevis told us that a fireman or policeman had come to warn him that the house might be surrounded by fire, and though it might be at a great distance, we might still find it anxious work sitting there, and possibly very difficult to get out from a ring of flame. He said we had better leave the house for the night, returning to it in the morning when the flames had either been mastered or had passed by us.

In the early afternoon, with a great deal of trouble Dr. Tevis had been able to secure a carriage with two horses. The driver had agreed to wait in front of the house until such time as we might need it. It was the only vehicle of any kind he could get, and masses of people had implored our host to allow them to use the carriage if only for a short distance. But he was adamant, as he knew that, at such time as it might be needed, it would be his only hope of transporting the two not strong enough to walk—Miss Fetridge and Madame Sembrich's Frieda—as well as of carrying our bare necessities.

On account of my apparent imperviousness and insensibility to the earthquake, Dr. Tevis, who could only think of others and their comfort, felt in me a sister soul, and asked my advice as to what we had better take with us for the night. Although we were panting from the excessive heat at the time, I counseled the taking of warm blankets and wraps—all that the carriage could hold—and a bottle of brandy. Why I should have foreseen the need of such comforters is curious; it seemed to have been an inspiration on my part.

As quickly as possible, therefore, our bags containing only a few valuables, together with a collection of blankets, coats and wraps, were put into the carriage with Miss Fetridge, and we started for North Beach, then a big stretch of vacant lots in the direction of Fort Mason. We had originally thought of going to the Presidio, but as it was at an enormous distance and we had to go on foot, we decided for the nearer place.

It was already dark when we got to North Beach, and it was certainly a long enough walk as it was. Some of our party kept all the time to the middle of the road, fearing more earthquake shocks or a falling chimney. I remember I was rather bored and thought it was a silly precaution.

One house we passed, within a block of the one we had left in Taylor Street, had had the front completely and precisely shorn off, leaving the whole of the interior in full view with the furniture jumbled together and strewn with plaster, looking like an old-fashioned doll's house in disorder. North Beach and its surroundings are not supposed to be the safest quarter of the city, so we arranged our blankets as near as possible to the road and lay down. The carriage was sent to wait on the other side so as not to call attention to us, as we had no idea what sort of people we had around us, and feared they might attack us for our valuables.

SOME MEMORIES AND REFLECTIONS

When we arrived we found the lots fully occupied. The ground made a hard and uncomfortable bed and, on account of the heavy dews, in spite of furs, a chilly one. I passed most of the night walking up and down. At intervals I would sleep from mere exhaustion for ten or fifteen minutes at a time in an agonized position of discomfort; then I would get up and walk about in order to throw off the chill. The dew fell upon us almost like rain, and the air was filled with falling soot and bits from the burning city. The road beside which we were camping was a highroad, a main thoroughfare between the city and Fort Mason.

Towards three o'clock in the morning some of our party went back to the house in Taylor Street to see how near the flames had come. My maid went with them to get a bag containing a change of linen for Miss Fetridge and me. They reported the flames to be within two blocks of the house, but creeping round the base of the hill still, and away from Dr. Tevis's house. We still hoped his large garden and vacant lots below would serve as a check to the flames.

Just at dawn and before sunrise, when there was a silvery blue light over everything and we were at our chilliest, a soldier in khaki came along and quietly asked us to move up the hill, as they were bringing along the prisoners, transferring them from the jail down town which had been partly demolished by the earthquake, to Fort Mason. About seventy-five of the most dazed-looking creatures, in two files, with lines of soldiers on either side, passed at a snail's pace in utter silence, hardly glancing about them. It was a dramatic moment in the chill of the morning, and what made it more impressive was their herd-like silence and the silence of all us refugees watching.

Smoke began to go up in little puffs here and there—people camped about us warming something for breakfast. The soldiers at once ordered all fires out.

During the night ownerless animals of various sorts prowled about, and Plançon, startled out of a stertorous nap to find a cow sniffing at his feet, awoke with the cry: *"Emma, quelle est cette horrible bête?"* (What is this horrible beast?) A flick of my handkerchief sent her away. It was rather a comfort to see the familiar animal, and also to see some dogs playing naturally. The earth was still there and we were on top of it instead of being engulfed.

At about seven o'clock that morning, a charming young woman, Mademoiselle de Bretteville, who lived in a house on the brow of the hill just above our encampment, came down to ask if we would like to go up to them for a cup of coffee and a rest, until we could decide what to do. She said she had, with her family, been watching the various encampments and seeing all the others were of a rough type, had had her curiosity aroused by our group and wished to save us discomfort if possible. Of course, we joyously accepted the idea of making ourselves less untidy.

The men of the party, Plançon and Dippel, were left to find the Opera Company by themselves, and Madame Sembrich, Miss Fetridge and I, accompanied by our maids, gratefully went up at once and, after making ourselves a little cleaner, sank on to the beds provided, to try and get an eyeful of sleep. Alas! We had hardly been lying down five minutes when Dr. Tevis came to call us and tell us he had been warned that we must get out of San Francisco if we could, as soon as possible.

We hastened to dress, then drank a cup of coffee and went back to the carriage. There we found the agent from Dr. Tevis's place in the country. He had come to town at once to look for the doctor, and had traced us after having been up to the house. He said the country house was badly damaged, too, and that the earthquake there (Alna, Santa Clara County) had been most severe. He thought, however, that, the fires having died down between us and the ferries, if we set off at once we could get across to Oakland, even taking the carriage with us; but that as the city was under martial law and there was no water and no bread, if we stayed there we ran the risk of all kinds of illnesses and discomforts and, later perhaps, of not even being able to take the carriage.

No idea of physical discomfort or fatigue entered my mind. Our only thought was to do what had to be done and not be a burden to anybody.

The horses were harnessed, and all the blankets, bags and wraps, including those we had worn in the night, were piled in and on the carriage. Miss Fetridge and Frieda got in, and the private secretary of our host, being armed, took his place on the box with the driver, as guard.

Our way led through the Barbary Coast, the

dwelling place of all the thieves and roughs of San Francisco. Those of the party going on foot set out by a way a little shorter than that to be taken by the carriage. All this time we were laughing and talking to keep up our courage, and probably from excitement and the fever of fatigue, although at the time one did not realize it. To see us, any one would have thought we were a pleasure party.

One great dramatic touch I learned first hand. People *in* a dramatic situation of great seriousness are so busy enduring it and facing it that they have not the time to be sorry for themselves, or to realize its extent.

The ground was very hot, being mostly pavements and cobblestones, and from having been chilled to the marrow in the night by the dew—which we could literally wring from the blankets—we were broiled by the heat; and as we walked the perspiration streamed from us, and our feet were almost blistered by the stones which had so recently been exposed to the ravaging heat of the fire.

They tell me we covered a distance of about six miles in that walk, although one was unconscious of every moment as it passed. I did not know whether I walked or flew those six miles—whether I was in the body or out of it.

We passed through a big square where, I was told, hundreds of victims were lying on the ground, dead, awaiting burial. Fortunately, I was warned in time not to look in that direction.

When we arrived at the ferry the carriage was not there, and we went through agony imagining every possible disaster that might have happened to it. After having waited a half hour that seemed an eternity, our host's secretary appeared to say he had misunderstood where they were to meet us, and they had been waiting about a mile away from the ferry at the end of Broadway, to see us pass. He at once rushed back and brought the carriage, and we boarded the ferry which, smelly and awful as it was, seemed heaven. Our whole desire was to get away with all possible haste from the stricken city where we should be bound to see agony and suffering we would be powerless to help.

In the saloon of the ferry, nectar and ambrosia awaited us in the shape of coffee and corned-beef hash. One could eat little, however, although the hot coffee was life-giving.

On arriving at Oakland Pier, Dr. Tevis decided to take us to the house of a cousin in Oakland, the quickest way to which was by train. So we put our two maids into the carriage to make the journey by road, while we took the shortest route. On arriving at Oakland, and after a walk of about ten or fifteen minutes, we reached the house, only to find it shut up and deserted, and no way of entering except by breaking in. Dr. Tevis wanted to do this, but we would not hear of it. The wife of his cousin, we learned, had been called to San José, where her father had been killed in the earthquake, and she had gone there at once.

Then our host set to work to find some sort of conveyance to take us up to his place in the mountains sixty miles away. All his efforts were in vain, until at last we saw a man arriving with a handful of tools. He had broken down in his automobile on coming from San José with the news of the death of Mrs. Tevis's father. He said if he could get his machine mended in time he could take us as far as San José, but, of course, that was not of much use. He said, however, he thought he could get two automobiles for us.

While he was talking, the carriage arrived with only my maid in it, Madame Sembrich's maid having been left behind with the Opera Company in Oakland through a misunderstanding. There had been a question of Madame Sembrich herself remaining at Oakland Ferry with the Opera Company, for whom a special train was being made up to take them back to New York, but she heard that the St. Francis Hotel was still standing, and she hoped to be able to get some of the clothes she had left there, to take away with her when she went east, and this had made her decide to wait with us. Her maid, who had been detained by the manager of the Opera Company pending Madame Sembrich's return from her stay with us, was immediately sent for, but after nearly two hours' wait the messenger we had sent came back, having been unable to trace her.

Madame Sembrich said she was wretched at the thought of retarding our departure, and she begged to be sent back to the Company, where she would ultimately find her maid and go back to New York at once. By that time, having learned that the St. Francis Hotel had been destroyed, we did not oppose her decision. So Dr. Tevis, Miss Fetridge, my maid and I got into another automobile that had been found, with our few bags, and set off on our sixty-mile drive. It was then after five o'clock in the afternoon.

By this time we were so tired and light-headed that our bodies no longer seemed to belong to us. I can say my spirit was sufficiently freed to be able to enjoy the scenery with my eyes bloodshot and aching and my head filled with fever. Beautiful California! The automobile was an open one, and we went so fast it was like flying.

Knowing that our friends in the East would be made most anxious by the sensational accounts of the earthquake, I promised Madame Sembrich I would send a telegram from the first place we passed where the wires were not down; but we found that all communications on the way had been severed. It was only little by little and by such signs, that one realized the extent and immensity of the disaster. One could not grasp it. I remember our saying, Dr. Tevis and I, "Now is the time when people whose souls are bound down by material possessions are going to suffer the most." It will ever be a source of thankfulness to me that I saw none of the agony or suffering I afterwards heard described.

When we got to San José we were stopped by the police and obliged to make a long detour, as the city was on fire and many streets blocked by ruins. It was appalling—or would have been had one been capable of feeling any amazement by that time—to see the houses in such a state of ruin; some shaken down like card houses, some twisted out of shape before collapsing, and some looking as though they had been sat upon.

By that time daylight was fading and we had to stop just beyond San José to ask our way and light our lamps. We did not even get out or think of stretching our legs. To get on was our one idea, and as quickly as possible, to the country and away from people and cities. Then we went on flying through the darkness, seeing only the light of our lamps, but getting whiffs of country air cool on our faces. At last we came to the entrance gates of Dr. Tevis's country place, from whence there was a steady climb of a mile over a road cut in the side of a mountain, with a sheer wall of rock on one side and a steep bank to the valley on the other. There were great fissures in this road caused by the earthquake, over which we bounded; and in some places the road was narrowed to danger limit by the landslides both upon and out of the road.

Finally we arrived at the last little incline of

about a hundred yards. The automobile would go no farther and we got out. There was a little circle of light on the plateau in front of the house, where a fire of logs was burning, and there the caretaker and his wife had set up their tent, not having dared to live under a roof since the first big shock. They had made themselves very comfortable, but the house was uninhabitable and the veranda surrounding it had collapsed entirely, although the walls were still standing.

Dr. Tevis's house stood directly over the "fault" and was irremediably damaged. It had been twisted round six inches on its foundations. Of course, all the plaster was down and hanging from the walls in ribbons; the front door of heavy oak two inches thick, although both bolted and barred, had been twisted off its hinges and thrown into the hall. All the glass was broken, and, of course, there was danger in going into the house, even for a night. Fortunately, the caretakers' house, which, in their fright, they had abandoned, was a little cottage all wood, even the walls and ceilings; and beyond broken windows and destroyed plumbing, no damage had been done to it. The floors were still covered with broken glass and crockery and everything

276

breakable, and they had not attempted to clear up the rubbish or put the place in order.

Dr. Tevis set everybody he could to work to clear it, and went himself to the big house to get blankets and sheets, towels and mattresses. Miss Fetridge and I had a room with two beds in it and space for little else. Dr. Tevis slept on the floor on a mattress in one room, and my maid in another.

Before we went to bed we had supper, the first morsel we had eaten since the coffee of the morning. It consisted of crackers, sardines and jam, as food, and a bottle of Pol Roger champagne, 1899 vintage. They had brought it from the house in San Francisco in case any body might be ill, but during the night out of doors it had been so cold that most of them took little sips of brandy when chilled through.

Of course, we had recurrent earthquake shocks all the time we were there in the country.

Afterwards we learned that the house in Taylor Street, San Francisco, was burning as we were on our way to the country. The chauffeur who had driven us up turned out to be a gentleman—a lawyer—who had lost

277

everything in the earthquake and fire, and the renting of his automobile had been his only way of obtaining some ready money for himself and his wife. Our host asked him to remain and rest, and go back the following day, but he left at once to do the sixty miles over again, as he said his wife must be anxious. Poor man! We heard afterwards that his machine had given out on the way back, and he had had to pass the night away from her, anyway. A poor reward for the gallant service he did us.

After the meager supper we had to go to bed *unwashed,* as there was no water we could get at; and I was reduced to such a pitch of degradation that I no longer cared whether I was dirty or not. Utter exhaustion had set in, and we slept like the dead.

The next morning I was awakened by the sunshine beating on the green shade of the window and etching thereon a beautiful rose vine which covered the little cottage. Hearing also the sound of running water, I felt an immediate desire to be clean, so took soap and towels and went out into the delicious morning air. By that time it was five-thirty. The caretaker's wife was there outside making a fire over some bricks set up on end to boil water for our coffee. I found a most beautiful mountain brook, full to the brim, running down through a grove near our little cottage. Telling the woman to look out that no people were about, I undressed and in the open air took an ice-cold bath in the stream itself. I felt like a new person, and that dear Mother Nature was indeed kind. A bath in the open air in water fresh from "Nature's fount" seemed to wash all the cobwebs away from my mind.

Even earthquakes seemed less fearful in the country, where one was far away from man's handiwork and inventions through which the great disaster had been rendered infinitely more devastating and hideous. A little shake and it was over. However, I don't know how it would have seemed to see the solid ground rolling like the waves of the sea, as they said it did.

After we had been to the house and chosen the few necessities for our daily life, and Dr. Tevis had in some measure organized the clearing up of his house and belongings, I walked with our host that day over miles of the place.

Fortunately, there was a plentifully supplied storeroom, and, as Dr. Tevis said, "the

279

hens had been kind enough to lay us a few eggs."

In our walk we found one of the mountain trails entirely blocked and discovered that the trail above had slipped down upon it.

One of the things done on that first day was to improvise a bathroom, and to this end a big galvanized iron tub was placed in the brook and covered with a tent.

Being so far away from the center we had no means of knowing what was happening in San Francisco or Oakland, and nobody knew what had become of us. At the end of four or five days during which there had been a frantic search for us, we managed to get into communication with the outside world by the aid of a telephone attached to a tree. Melville Stone, then head of the Associated Press, at once got into touch with me and asked me to write a short account of my experiences. This I did.

Through my article for the Associated Press the transportation agents of the Opera Company learned where I was, and made the necessary arrangements to take us back East.

By that time I knew the San Francisco house was in ashes, with all it contained, including our twenty-seven trunks. So I arranged with the agent to go East on the Wednesday of the following week, for both my friend and I were too exhausted to anticipate that five-day journey without an interval of rest.

The day after we had settled in the farmhouse Dr. Tevis's agent had brought us news of the fire. On their way to Van Ness Avenue the flames had spared Nob Hill, only to sweep back upon it at a sudden change of wind. The servants had had barely time to bury the silver, a head of Minerva by Rodin, and one or two more of Dr. Tevis's particular treasures, and to take his beautiful collection of Keith paintings out of their frames and carry them to safety before the fire was upon them. When I visited Nob Hill again in 1915, I found that Dr. Tevis had made no effort to rebuild, neither had he sold the land, and all one saw of that once charming house and its innumerable treasures was two charred gateposts.

As soon as we heard the house was gone we saw there was no use waiting. We had still thought to save our belongings, that being one reason for our not joining the Opera Company and going East with them, though a second reason was that it was doubtful, at the time, whether their train would start at all, or having started, would get through. We were days waiting for this question of our departure to be settled, and it was finally arranged for us to leave on Friday, April 27.

I think that week of life in the open air, with exercise and very little food, was the best thing that could have happened to us, although we chafed at the delay. A shock of sorts the earthquake certainly must have been to me even while I was unconscious of fear or even nervousness, for once away from it and in the country with no effort to be made, I was unable to make a sound for three days, unable even to speak, as though the nerves of my throat had been paralyzed.

The morning of our departure it was pouring. We had to leave at dawn and drive through the rain to Los Gatos, taking there a narrow gauge railway to Oakland. By tramway we went on to another station and took another train to the pier, where we were to board the eastbound train. There the Union Pacific agent did not find our tickets, as he had expected, and had to cross over the ferry to San Francisco to get them. For us it was rather a nervous moment for fear he would not return in time.

When he did arrive and we were safely on

the train, it is difficult to describe adequately our feelings of relief and gratitude. Before leaving Oakland we looked back across the bay at the heap of ruins that was once San Francisco, where thousands of undaunted, courageous men were already hard at work organizing help for those less fortunate, and already rebuilding their city.

It was worth going through an earthquake to see such fortitude, bravery and unselfishness as San Francisco's trouble brought out in her children. I cannot find words to express my admiration for them.

VIII

WE arrived in New York minus all of our clothing and the costumes for three operas. We had nothing but the clothes in which we stood. Fortunately, I had left one evening dress in New York, with the intention of discarding it upon my return. Instead, I resurrected it to very good purpose, and wore it at a big concert given for the benefit of the firemen of New York. Having just come from the San Francisco disaster, it was only appropriate that I should do something for those who fight fire. At the end of my last number a squad of the tallest and huskiest firemen on the force marched on to the stage from both wings and presented me with huge bouquets that literally weighed me down.

Almost immediately after my arrival in New York I received a cable from Mrs. Whitelaw Reid, whose husband was then the United States Ambassador in London, asking me to sing at a party they were giving for King Edward not quite a fortnight after the date set for my arrival in Paris. I accepted at once, and cabled Worth to get a dress ready for me. I had scarcely time to arrive in Paris, be fitted and get to London before the evening of Mrs. Reid's party. Caruso and Gilibert were on the program with me that night, but I'm ashamed to say I have forgotten the name of the contralto. There was one, however, for we ended the program with the quartet from "Rigoletto."

This was the first time that I had seen King Edward since his accession to the throne, and when I made my appearance it seemed good to see his face light up with the same cordial, kindly, friendly smile of the Prince of Wales period and to note his evident pleasure in my singing.

He sent for me at once when the concert was concluded and expressed his great pleasure at seeing me again. Then he said: "But you don't look like an earthquake sufferer. Worth, I am sure, is responsible for that dress."

In the course of the conversation that followed he asked suddenly: "Why do you never sing for us any more? Is it because you despise us, as I have been told?"

I replied: "Not exactly, but rather because I like my last baby best."

He, not understanding immediately, said: "But you have no children. What do you mean?"

"Do you remember 'Aïda,' sir," I answered, "and the fact that it was the best thing I had done that far?"

"Yes."

"Well, I have sung 'Tosca' since, and she is my pet at present. As I am not permitted to sing 'Tosca' in London, I prefer not to sing at all."

He looked rather troubled at this, and said: "We'll see about that."

Nothing ever came of his remark, however, as I could have foretold. Not even the King of England could have prevailed upon the singer who had prevented my début in Brussels and who had hurried to buy the London rights to "Tosca" immediately after my success therein, to relinquish them to a rival singer, and least of all to me.

After the concert I was taken in to supper by the Duke of Manchester. The refreshments were served at little tables on the floor below the music room, and the one at which I sat was directly next to that of the King. His Majesty was perfectly delightful all the evening, talking across from his table to me through the whole supper. This was the last time I ever saw him.

While I was in London, a friend begged me to go to an evening party given in honor of the Princess Christian, who had expressed herself as most anxious to hear about the earthquake. I went to the party, told the Princess Christian about the disaster, had a long, interesting chat with her, and then, feeling that I had fulfilled my social obligations and that nothing more could be expected of me, I left immediately, to the utter disgust of my friend, who had evidently planned on my seeing the party through.

I made a flying trip to Paris, and then returned to London to sing at a large party given by Mrs. John Mackay. I then followed Julian to Italy, where he had gone on ahead to await me. This was my last summer in Italy.

In the winter of 1906-07 I added "Trovatore" to my repertoire. This I sang with Caruso and, frankly, enjoyed very much. Both "Trovatore" and "Ballo in Maschera," written, as they were, in the ancient mode, I found tremendously restful to the nerves and the motions. Even "Tosca," which puts no strain on the mind of a singer, is not so easy to sing, as it is very exhausting, emotionally and temperamentally.

I enjoyed singing with Caruso immensely. Of peasant origin, he had the simplicity and lovableness of a child. His was indeed a heart of gold and a voice of gold, and of all the tenors with whom I have ever sung, I have never known one kinder, more amiable or readier to play fair with his vis-á-vis on the stage. Some others with whom I have appeared during my career devoted their entire time and energy to maneuvering for the spot on the stage most propitious to their voices, and so intriguing as to place their comrades in such positions as would compel them to sing into the wings.

Mr. Conried followed Mr. Grau in letting me choose whatever new opera I might wish to add to my repertoire. When, therefore, he offered me "Butterfly," I begged him to produce "Iris" by Mascagni instead, and he gave way gracefully.

I had seen and studied the score of "Iris," and although the story was not without its painful moments, it was so exquisitely poetic and so consistently Japanese—which "Butterfly" is not—that I knew I could make something of it. I also felt that, as it entailed

Photograph by Aimé Dupont

AS IRIS

a minimum of action, it would be an excellent medium for a demonstration of my theory that thought, clearly directed, has a greater power of moving an audience than any theatricality of gesture.

As I knew that the interpretation of such a rôle as Iris must be preceded by a minute study of Japanese gesture, costume and attitude, I appealed to Madame Waddington, and she was kind enough to make an appointment for me with the Japanese ambassador in order that I might ask him to direct me to some one who could instruct me in all matters Nipponese. He told me, to my delight, that the greatest of Japanese actresses, Sada Yacco—whom I remembered having met in Boston years before when her company was making its first American tour—was living in Paris at that time, and studying the Occidental theater and its methods, so as to be able to introduce them later into the new theater then being built at Tokyo; and that undoubtedly she would have ample time to help me should she be willing to do so. He invited her to the Embassy to meet me, and at the same time put one of the secretaries at my disposal as interpreter. It turned out that Sada Yacco remembered me perfectly, and was most amiable and delighted to help me.

I went several times to her charming little place in the Villa Montmorency, where she had quite a household, which was ruled by several perfectly enchanting little sleeve dogs, or papillons, as they are called here. During my visits to her she illustrated, at my request, the various emotions I was called upon to express in "Iris," and as she did so I studied her every attitude, her every movement, or lack of movement, and registered her Oriental atmosphere.

The rôle was permitted hardly any gestures, every effect being by the attitude of the body, and every emotion conveyed by the voice and its inflections. In the scene where her father accuses Iris unjustly and bespatters her with mud, she has to stand motionless upon a little table where her lover has placed her the better to admire her, the expression of her face and the attitude of her body alone giving any indication of her breaking heart. And the final scene depends wholly upon the expressiveness of the voice as she sings her last phrases from the darkness of the drain in which she has thrown herself to die.

Sada Yacco lent me her dresses and even her obis—an obi is a sacred treasure to a Jap-

anese woman—in order that I might have
them copied in my size by Madame Landolf,
of whom I have previously spoken. She also
allowed me to dress and undress her endless
times as though she were a doll, so that I
might learn to tie the obi as do the Japanese.

My costumes, when they were completed,
were Oriental to the last detail. Each gar-
ment was tied with strings, and there was
nothing so European as a button or snap or
hook and eye on one of them. I chose my doll
with the idea of its making me look smaller
without at the same time buying one that
would seem strikingly larger than the average.
Proportion in everything always was my aim.
Also, singing the opera as I did with Caruso
and Scotti, who were large men, helped me to
look little. Both these artists were superla-
tive in their rôles.

Sada Yacco even made me up so that I
might correct the lines of my own face and yet
give it the Japanese cast of features. This
make-up I changed later in one item. She had
painted my face a blue white, which is all very
well for a dark skin, but looks ghastly on a
fair one. Instead of the blue white, I used a
very dark cream color. My eyes and nose
were painted in such a way as to make my

eyes seem smaller and my nose flattened, and my whole appearance was so changed by the make-up and costumes that my mother told me it was only when I turned full profile to the audience that she was able to recognize me.

After I had appeared in this rôle I had many letters from Japanese people thanking me for giving such a correct and consistent portrayal of a real Japanese maiden.

It was this winter that I lost my most beloved little dog, Peeny. I was singing in "Dona Anna," which was a new addition to my repertoire that year, and although Mahler, who conducted, was most kind and understanding, I took no joy in the performance, nor did I give it the strength and authority which I could otherwise have brought to it. My treasured little companion was dying on the night of the first performance, and I was quite heartbroken at the thought of her imminent loss. Only those who have the real love and understanding of animals can realize how my grief overwhelmed me.

Towards the end of the season Mr. Conried resigned, his health having broken down, and the administration of the Metropolitan Opera Company was put provisionally in the hands of Mr. Dippel.

Among the many candidates considered for Mr. Conried's post were several of the local managers in cities which the company had visited on its annual spring tours. But a certain small clique among the box-holders were determined to bring to the Metropolitan Gatti-Casazza and Toscanini, who had unquestionably been most successful in their administration at La Scala in Milan.

However, in spite of the record these two Italians had made at La Scala, I felt that with their different ideas and psychology they would destroy everything that Maurice Grau and Conried had labored so hard to build up, and that whatever practical or commercial good might come of their régime would be offset by the change in operatic ideals.

Therefore, while their engagement was still hanging fire, I went to Pierpont Morgan and begged him to use his influence to keep intact the fine traditions established by Maurice Grau at the Metropolitan, and to see that the direction of the Company was put in the hands of some one who had watched the growth of the Metropolitan and knew and understood and respected these traditions. He was most charming, and told me that he would do everything in his power to carry out my wishes provided I was going to remain with the Company. But I told him that I felt I was getting to the end of my career and that, although Mr. Dippel, who was empowered to make contracts, had asked me to sign for three more years, I had refused, partly because I believed that the time for my retirement was near, and partly because I knew that, should Gatti-Casazza become director of the opera, I should never be able to endure the atmosphere he and Toscanini would bring with them. When Mr. Morgan learned that I had no intention to remain longer than one more year with the Company, he declared himself too busy to bother with affairs at the Metropolitan.

My attitude towards the Gatti-Casazza-Toscanini combination was not born of an idle whim or any personal animosity, but of a perfect understanding of Italian operatic ideals and the attitude of those in power towards the artists. In Italy, singers are knocked about like dogs—indeed, the slang phrase for them is "cane," and the house of rest and retreat Verdi in his will provided for them in Milan is, in Italian, called the "House of Dogs." Their social status is that of mummers of Shakespeare's time; a few years ago the son of one of the greatest Italian singers who ever

EMMA EAMES IN HER GARDEN AT BATH, MAINE

EMMA EAMES AND "BETTY," BATH, MAINE

lived and who was worshiped in America, begged to be taken away from the school in which his father had placed him, saying he could not endure the brutal contempt with which his comrades treated him because his father was an opera singer.

In addition to their belief that artists belong to a lower order of beings, the Italians do not feel that intellect or education, even musical education, is necessary to the singer. One of the greatest of the Italian singers—a natural and instinctive operatic interpreter—does not read a note of music, does not own one score of an opera, and has been taught all his rôles by ear! Therefore, as they are supposed to have neither intellect nor nerves nor feelings, they are regarded as pawns in the operatic game by the Gatti-Casazzas. They are called upon to rehearse at any and all hours; they are turned on and off like talking-machine records; and great interpretative art—except in the case of a miracle singer like Caruso—is not born of such conditions.

In Italy—I am speaking now of the nineties and early nineteen-hundreds—a well-rounded characterization in which brains, musical feeling and imagination played as important parts as vocal accomplishments, instinct and purely elemental expression, was the greatest exception and never expected except in rare cases.

The reason "Tosca" is such a rest to an artist who is a conscientious singing actress is because it is written for the instinctive singers of the Italian school, and its intention and appeal are elemental. But the French school, of which we were exponents, as well as the classic German school, demanded more than a natural voice and temperament. They demanded artistic distinction. And incidentally, the Italian singers who came to the Metropolitan under Grau either acquired this distinction, not only of interpretation but of appearance, dress and deportment, or else they fell out.

The reason Gounod refused to accept the Italian singer chosen by Gaillard as his Juliet in 1889 was because she did not have this quality, and therefore could not be as one with the French singers with whom she would be called upon to appear.

It is true that the French, in their insistence upon this aristocratic tradition of artistry, sometimes leaned a little backwards. They sacrificed pure vocal beauty to diction or the clearness of the words. Especially before the

War, the French method of voice production gave a tone that sounded a little pinched and hard, at least to our ears. In the last two or three years, since my return to Paris, I have been both amazed and delighted to notice a change for the better in vocal production and generosity of tone, particularly at the Opéra Comique, without, however, sacrificing the clearness of diction.

The summer following my audience with Pierpont Morgan I learned that the Italians, Gatti-Casazza and Toscanini, had been definitely engaged; and knowing I could not do myself justice under the conditions and atmosphere they would create about them, upon my return to America in the autumn I quietly told the reporters who met me at the pier, that it would be my last season. As a matter of fact, even under the most favorable conditions I was finding it increasingly difficult to gather strength for my public appearances.

Almost immediately after I had announced my intention, Madame Sembrich made the same announcement with regard to herself. She organized a big farewell at the opera and her devoted friends and admirers gave her a sumptuous farewell dinner, at which I was glad to be present and to add my tribute of homage to a great artist, musician and treasured friend.

In my contract I had stipulated that I should have three performances of "Iris" that last season, but Toscanini refused to conduct it or permit it to be presented again. Naturally, this was a great disappointment to me, but as it was my last year I did nothing to force the issue.

Gatti-Casazza declared my contract to be a constant stumbling-block in his path. I retorted that it was the only definite and orderly thing in his administration, which, by the way, was ruled entirely by the temperament of that great conductor Toscanini. As an operatic conductor he left much to be desired by comparison with such great ones as Seidl and Mancinelli. He was charming and amiable, and rehearsed at the piano with me, taking all my shades and intentions. Once before the public, however, the opera was his and his alone. He had such a marvelous and exact memory that he could reproduce always what he had heard one do at any one particular rehearsal, and only that. He detached himself from us thereafter and interpreted his opera, even singing with us so loudly that one heard him on the stage.

SOME MEMORIES AND REFLECTIONS

Even to such as ourselves, who had an absolute respect for the music as it was written, he allowed no margin for the emotion of the moment, and his conducting was not an accompaniment but a stone wall of resistance to any personality but his own. This is all very well in a symphony conductor, but does not make for the ease and freedom necessary for the interpretation of those who have anything really to give and the authority to communicate it. Caruso and I discussed this and he was absolutely in accord with me in regard to these reasons for the difficulty of singing with Toscanini.

Under Gatti-Casazza's rule, one knew hardly from one day to the next when one would be called upon to sing. It was quite evident that the Italian combination not only believed that one lived in the theater like the janitor, but that one could be turned on and off at will, an attitude which obviously did not make for the comfort of an artist accustomed to the order and balance maintained in the organization by Maurice Grau and his successor, Mr. Conried.

The lack of a logical system on the part of the new management was a source of great annoyance to me for two reasons. First, no matter how many times I had sung a rôle, and no matter how many years it had been a successful part of my repertoire, I never wanted to present it without going over it carefully the day preceding its performance. Second, certain operas tired me more than others. It was easier, for instance, for me to sing the "Nozze di Figaro" followed by "Aïda," than it was to sing "Aïda" succeeded by the "Nozze di Figaro." These two simple things make all the difference in the world in the merit of a performance. But sequence was a thing impossible to foresee or control under the new direction.

However, I said nothing, as it was my last season, although I do not believe that any one realized I meant what I said when I stated that I was not returning.

When I had announced my imminent retirement, Dr. Jacoby, who had seen me through so much illness, begged me to reconsider my decision and to go on with my career even if I left the Metropolitan, saying that the idea of my retiring at forty-three was not only absurd, but that I would find inactivity maddening after my busy life.

In a way he was right, as the break with the work of a lifetime proved an almost unbearable one to me. A career is a wonderful and terrible thing. If one thought of the pain, the frustration, the discontent, "divine" though it may be, one would feel the game of such a life not worth the candle. But the joy of accomplishment more than outweighs such drawbacks. The sense of exaltation and expansion that follows the establishment of a perfect vibration between an artist and his public, brings one nearer heaven than anything else on earth. The vibrations of a *grande passion* are the only ones that can be compared with it, but these, alas! are shared with another and dependent upon that other; the artistic passion frees one, and is therefore complete and infinitely more satisfactory.

When I have said in these pages that I regarded singing as an adjunct, I did not mean to convey that singing was not a great joy to me. It was. Often, and especially after months of imposed silence, the mere sound of my voice and the sensation of its vibrations in my throat, moved me to choking tears, happy tears. No, my leaving the stage was not an easy thing.

One day, not long ago, I was speaking of this retirement and, without realizing what I had said until my attention was called to it,

I stated, not, "I stopped singing in 1909," but, "I died in 1909."

Every artist dies twice, and the first time, the death of one's activities, is the most painful. I realized this for the first time after my breakdown just succeeding the "Tosca" revival, when it suddenly came to me that my only source of real happiness lay in my career.

But I had made a resolution early in life not to continue singing in opera after I was forty. I knew that my voice and my whole temperament were suited to the interpretation of romantic, lyric, poetic, young heroines, and therefore, when I was forty-three and a half years old, I retired.

To continue at the Metropolitan under the Italian régime would have been impossible to one of my artistic ideals; to seek new fields at my age of fixed habits would have been to court disaster—the very thought of it chilled me; to confront and win a new public would have been an effort beyond my strength; to repeat myself in operas that I had brought to the highest degree of development of which I was capable would have been an anti-climax, and would have ended by boring me; to undertake any of the heavier rôles of the Wagnerian repertoire I had proved beyond the shadow of

EMMA EAMES DE GOGORZA

a doubt would have been beyond my powers. Therefore, the logical moment had come for me to say good-by, when my public had only my successes to remember. If I had gone on they would regretfully have said—as they have of others—"How lovely she was. What a pity she did not retire sooner." Now I have no regrets, as I brought my career to a close at its apogee.

During the last years of my operatic career and after the success of my big concert tour, I always sang a few concerts each spring and autumn succeeding and preceding the opera season. Emilio de Gogorza was often engaged to sing with me, as our duets had given so much pleasure on our first tour. On one of these concert tours we inaugurated the beautiful Temple of Arts at Bar Harbor.

My last performance at the Metropolitan was in "Tosca." Those were the days when one received twenty-five curtain calls, and the lights had to be put out in order to prevail upon the people to leave the house. That night, my last, the audience was one of the most demonstrative of that enthusiastic period, and at the end of the performance demanded a speech of me. And it was then I told them:

"I wish to tell you that this is the last time

I shall sing for you. But before I go I want to thank you for all you have done to help me to do better work and make the best of myself, to thank you for your inspiration and for the fact that I have felt that you loved me and delighted in my success. Good-by!"

THE END

INDEX

INDEX

306

INDEX

Index

INDEX

309

INDEX

INDEX

(1)

The Recordings of EMMA EAMES (13 Aug., 1865 - 13 Jun., 1952)

A DISCOGRAPHY

by W. R. Moran

Honorary Curator, Archive of Recorded Sound, Stanford University

I. "The MAPLESON CYLINDERS": Non-commercial recordings of fragments of actual performances at the Metropolitan Opera House, New York, made by Librarian Lionel Mapleson on two-minute wax cylinders. All catalog numbers refer to transfers made to 78 rpm or Lp discs. The quality of these recordings is excruciatingly bad, but they are of considerable historical interest, especially to the serious vocal student.

Discog. No.	Date	78 rpm issues	Lp issues
1.	TOSCA: Ah!... mostro... Lo strazi, lo uccidi! (Torture scene, Act II) (Puccini) (w. Emilio De Marchi (t) & Antonio Scotti (bar)) (w. Or: cond. by Luigi Mancinelli)		
	3 Jan. '03	IRCC 179; 3057	IRCC L-7004
2.	TOSCA: Portatelo qui... Vittoria! Vittoria! (Torture scene, Act II) (Puccini) (w. De Marchi & Scotti) (Or. Mancinelli)		
	3 Jan. '03	IRCC 179; 3057	IRCC L-7004
3.	TOSCA: Sempre con fè sincera (a fragment of Vissi d'arte) (Act II) (Puccini) (Or. Mancinelli)		
	3 Jan. '03	--------	IRCC L-7004
*4.	TOSCA: Com' è bello il mio Mario! (Finale, Act III) (Puccini) (w. Jacques Bars (t) & Bernard Bégué (bs.) (Or. Mancinelli)		
	3 Jan. '03	IRCC 216; 3057	IRCC L-7004

II. VICTOR TALKING MACHINE CO., Camden, N.J. & New York. 12" Red Seal

Discog. No.	Matrix-Take	Date	s/face Cat.No.	d/face Cat.No.	HMV s/face	HMV d/face	"78" rpm reissues	Re-recordings on Lp discs	Speed of original
5.	a) Als die Mutter (Dvorak, Op. 55, No. 4); b) Meine Liebe ist grün (F. Schumann-J. Brahms, Op. 63, No. 5) (G) (Pf.)								
	C-6207-1,-2	19 May, '08	------	------	------	------	------	------	
6.	Ave Maria (Meditation on Bach's Prelude, WTC-1 - Ch. F. Gounod) (Latin) (Pf.)								
	C-2318-1	20 Feb. '05	85054 / 88007	------	------	------	------	------	78.26 rpm
7.	Ave Maria (Bach-Gounod) (L) (Pf. & 'cello by Josef Hollman)								
	C-3076-1	1 Feb. '06	85098 / 88016	6088	03067	DB 430	------	------	77.43
8.	CARMEN: Je dis que rien ne m'épouvante (Micaela's air) (Bizet) (F) (Or.)								
	C-3386-1	14 May, '06	88036	------	033020	------	IRCC 32 / AGSB 60	Rococo 29	76.00
*9.	CAVALLERIA RUSTICANA: Voi lo sapete, o Mamma (Mascagni) (I) (Or.)								
	C-3388-1,-2	14 May, '06	88037	------	053092	------	------	Rococo 29	76.00
*10.	CAVALLERIA RUSTICANA: Voi lo sapete, o Mamma (Mascagni) (I) (Or. & Harp)								
	C-4034-1	13 Nov. '06	------	------	------	------	------	------	76.60
	-2	16 Nov. '06	88037	------	053092	------	IRCC 90	------	
11.	Chanson d'amour (Hollman) (F) (Pf. & 'cello by Josef Hollman)								
	C-3074-1	1 Feb. '06	85097 / 88015	------	033019	DB 648	------	------	77.43
12.	Chanson des baisers (Hermann Bemberg) (F) (Pf.)								
	C-6206-1	19 May, '08	88133	------	------	------	IRCC 90 / AGSB 5	Rococo 29	72.73
*13.	CHÉRUBIN: Viva amour (Aubade): See "Si tu le veux" (Discography No. 45)								
	Crucifix (Fauré) (Or.) (w. Emilio de Gogorza)								
	C-3172-1,-2	9 Mar. '06	89004	------	034000	------	------	------	76.60
	-3	22 May, '07	89004	------	------	------	------	------	78.26
	-4	6 Apr. '09	89004	------	------	------	------	------	75.00

Dixie (Dan D. Emmett): See "Star Spangled Banner" (Discography No. 47)

No.	Title / Matrix / Date					rpm
*14.	DON GIOVANNI: Là ci darem la mano (Mozart) (I) (w. Emilio de Gogorza) (Pf. & 'cello by Josef Hollman) C-3077-1 1 Feb. '06	(85099)	------	------	------	
*15.	DON GIOVANNI: Là ci darem la mano (Mozart) (I) (w. Emilio de Gogorza) (Or.) C-3170-1,-2 9 Mar. '06	89005	054071	IRCC 20	------	76.60
*16.	DON GIOVANNI: Là ci darem la mano (Mozart) (I) (w. Emilio de Gogorza) (Or.) C-4263-1 22 May, '07	89005	------	------	------	78.26
17.	Dopo! (F. Paolo Tosti) (I) (Or.) C-11307-1 27 Nov. '11	88344	------	IRCC 43 / AGSB 5	Rococo 29	76.60
18.	a) Early Morning (Peel); b) Prelude (Bloch) (E) (Pf. Henri Gilles) C-11313-1 27 Nov. '11	------	------	------		
19.	Élégie (Gallet-Massenet) (Based on the Invocation from "Les Erinnyes") (F) (Pf. & Violin) C-2402-1 16 Mar. '05	85063 / 88014	033014	------		79.13
20.	Élégie (Gallet-Massenet) (F) (Pf. & 'cello by Josef Hollman) C-3075-1 1 Feb. '06	88014	6088	------		77.43
21.	FAUST: Il était un roi de Thulé (Gounod) (F) (Or.) C-4066-1 27 Nov. '06	88045	033024	------		77.43
22.	FAUST: Ah! Je ris de me voir (Air des bijoux) (Gounod) (F) (Pf.) C-2317-1 20 Feb. '05	85053 / 88006	033013	HRS 1016	Rococo 29	78.26
23.	FAUST: Ah! Je ris de me voir (Air des bijoux) (Gounod) (F) (Or.) C-4049-1 16 Nov. '06	88006	033023	------		76.60
24.	FAUST: Alerte! alerte! ou vous êtes perdus! (Gounod) (F) (Or.) (w. Charles Dalmores & Pol Plançon) C-4332-1,-2 25 Mar. '07	95300	034015	HRS 1016	------	77.43
25.	IL FALUTO MAGICO: La dove prende (Zauberflöte: Bei Männern) (Mozart) (I) (Or.) (w. Emilio de Gogorza) C-3171-1,-2,-3 9 Mar. '06	89003 8043	054072 DK 121	AGSB 15	------	76.60

79.13 rpm

26. Goodbye! (F. Paolo Tosti) (E) (Pf.)
    C-2400-1,-2   16 Mar. '05   85058   ------   DB 648   03043   ------   ------   Rococo 29   ------   79.13 rpm
                                  88009

27. Gretchen am Spinnrade (Goethe-Schubert, D. 118) (G) (Pf. Henri Gilles)
    C-11312-1   27 Nov. '11   ------   ------   ------   ------   IRCC 76   ------
          -2   28 Nov. '11   88367   ------   ------   ------   AGSB 22   Rococo 29   76.60

28. HAMLET: Doute de la lumière (Thomas) (F) (Or.) (w. Emilio de Gogorza)
    C-3387-1   14 May, '06   ------   ------   ------   ------   ------   ------

29. LES HUGUENOTS: Nobles Seigneurs, salut! (Meyerbeer) (F) (Or.)
    C-6234-1   26 May, '08   ------   ------   ------   ------   ------   ------

30. a) L'Incrédule (Verlaine-R. Hahn) (F); b) The Year's at the Spring (Browning-Mrs. H.H.A. Beach) (E) (Pf.)
    C-2314-1   20 Feb. '05   85057   ------   ------   ------   ------   ------
          -2   16 Mar. '05   88008   03041   ------   IRCC 125   Rococo 29 (b only) 79.13

I Once had a Sweet little Doll, Dears (Nevin): See "Love in May" (Discography No. 34)

It was a Lover and his Lass (Shakespeare-Walthew): See "Véronique: Trot Here, Trot There" (Discography No. 55)

31. LAKMÉ: Viens, Mallika, les lianes en fleurs... Dôme épais le jasmin (Delibes) (F) (Pf.) (w. Louise Homer)
    C-6209-1   20 May, '08   ------   ------   ------   ------   ------   ------

32. LAKMÉ: Viens, Mallika, les lianes en fleurs... Dôme épais le jasmin (Delibes) (F) (Or.) (w. Louise Homer)
    C-6225-1,-2   25 May, '08   89020   034026   ------   IRCC 44   Rococo 29   75.00

33. LOHENGRIN: Du Aermste kannst wohl (Wagner) (G) (Or.) (w. Louise Homer)
    C-6226-1   25 May, '08   89021   044090   ------   IRCC 44   ------   75.00

34. a) Love in May (Horatio Parker); b) I Once had a Sweet little Doll, Dears (Ethelbert Nevin) (E) (Pf.)
    C-6201-1   18 May, '08   88131   ------   ------   IRCC 194   ------   72.73

35. MADAMA BUTTERFLY: Un bel dì vedremo (Puccini) (I) (Or.)
    C-11310-1   27 Nov. '11   ------   ------   ------   ------   ------

Meine Liebe ist grün (J. Brahms, Op. 63, No. 5): See "Als die Mutter" (Discography No. 5)

No.	Title / Matrix — Date						rpm
36.	Musica Proibita (Stanislao Gastaldon) (I) (Or.) C-11308-1 27 Nov. '11	------					75.00
37.	LE NOZZE DI FIGARO: Crudel, perchè finora (Mozart) (I) (Or.) (w. Emilio de Gogorza) C-6232-1 26 May, '08	------	------				
38.	LE NOZZE DI FIGARO: Crudel, perchè finora (Mozart) (I) (Or.) (w. Emilio de Gogorza) C-6967-1,-2 6 Apr. '09	89023		IRCC 20			
39.	LE NOZZE DI FIGARO: Dove sono (Mozart) (I) (Pf.) C-2420-1 28 Mar. '05	------					
40.	LE NOZZE DI FIGARO: Sull' aria!... che soave zeffiretto (Mozart) (I) (Or.) (w. Marcella Sembrich) C-3364-1,-2 5 May, '06	------					
41.	LE NOZZE DI FIGARO: Sull' aria!...che soave zeffiretto (Mozart) (I) (Or.) (w. Marcella Sembrich) C-5040-1,-2,-3 25 Jan. '08	95202 8043	054200 2-054100	DK 121	Rococo 29		81.82
*42.	OTELLO: Ave Maria (Verdi) (I) (Or.) C-3385-1,-2 14 May, '06 -3,-4 27 Nov. '06	------ ------	053091 ------	IRCC 125 ------	Rococo 29 ------		76.00 77.43
	Prelude (Bloch): See "Early Morning" (Discography No. 18)						
43.	ROMEO ET JULIETTE: Je veux vivre dans ce rêve (Valse) (Gounod) (F) (Pf.) C-2419-1 28 Mar. '05	85060 88011	033015	------			79.13
44.	ROMEO ET JULIETTE: Je veux vivre dans ce rêve (Valse) (Gounod) (F) (Or.) C-4032-1 13 Nov. '06	88011	033022	IRCC 43			76.60
45.	a) Si tu le veux (Charles Koechlin); b) CHÉRUBIN: Viva amour (Aubade) (Massenet) (F) (Pf.) C-6202-1 18 May, '08	88135	------	IRCC 76 AGSB 60	Rococo 29		72.73
*46.	a) Spring (Sir George Henschel); b) The Year's at the Spring (Browning-Mrs. H.H.A. Beach) (E) (Pf.) C-6203-1 18 May, '08	88008	------	IRCC 194 AGSB 22			72.73

*47. a) The Star Spangled Banner (Francis Scott Key–Samuel Arnold); b) Dixie (Dan D. Emmett) (E) (Pf.)

Matrix / Take	Date	Cat.	Victor	Reissue	rpm
C-2421-1,-2	28 Mar. '05	03044	85061 / 88012	Rococo 29 (b only)	79.13 rpm

48. Still wie die Nacht (Karl Böhm) (G) (Pf.)

Matrix / Take	Date	Cat.	Victor	Reissue	rpm
C-2315-1	20 Feb. '05	043058	85052 / 88005	------	78.26

49. Still wie die Nacht (Karl Böhm) (G) (Or.)

Matrix / Take	Date	Cat.	Victor	Reissue	rpm
C-4067-1	27 Nov. '06	------	88005	------	77.43

50. TOSCA: Vissi d'arte, vissi d'amore (Puccini) (I) (Pf.)

Matrix / Take	Date	Cat.	Victor	Reissue	rpm
C-2401-1	16 Mar. '05	053058	85059 / 88010	IRCC 32 / Rococo 29	79.13

51. TOSCA: Vissi d'arte, vissi d'amore (Puccini) (I) (Or.)

Matrix / Take	Date	Cat.	Victor	Reissue	rpm
C-4033-1,-2	13 Nov. '06	------	------	------	
-3	16 Nov. '06	------	------	------	
-4,-5	25 Jan. '08	------	88010	------	81.82

52. IL TROVATORE: Mira d'acerbe lagrime... Vivra! Contende il giubilo (Verdi) (I) (Or.) (w. Emilio de Gogorza)

Matrix / Take	Date	Cat.	Victor	Reissue	rpm
C-6233-1,-2	26 May, '08	------	------	------	
-3	6 Apr. '09	------	------	------	
-4,-5	7 Apr. '09	------	89022	IRCC 113 / AGSB 15	75.00

*53. Vents Furieux (Ariette) (Jean Philippe Rameau) (F) (Or.)

Matrix / Take	Date	Cat.	Victor	Reissue	rpm
B-11316-1	28 Nov. '11	------	(87106)	------	

*54. VÉRONIQUE: You are laughing, now tell me why (The Swing Song) (Eldes-Greenbank-Messager) (E) (Or.) (w. de Gogorza)

Matrix / Take	Date	Cat.	Victor	Reissue	rpm
C-11309-1	27 Nov. '11	------	89063	------	76.60

55. a) VÉRONIQUE: Trot here, trot there (Eldes-Greenbank-Messager); b) It was a Lover and his Lass (Shakespeare-Walthew) (E) (Pf. by Henri Gilles) (w. Emilio de Gogorza)

Matrix / Take	Date	Cat.	Victor	Reissue	rpm
C-11311-1	27 Nov. '11	------	------	------	

56. Who is Sylvia? (Shakespeare-Schubert, D. 891) (E) (Pf.)

Matrix / Take	Date	Cat.	Victor	Reissue	rpm
C-2316-1	20 Feb. '05	03045 / 03673	85062 / 88013	DB 430	79.13
-2	28 Mar. '05	------	------	------	

The Year's at the Spring: See "L'Incrédule" (Discography No. 30) also <u>"Spring"</u> (Discography No. 46)

ZAUBERFLÖTE (Mozart): See "Il Flauto Magico" (Discography No. 25)

III. INTERNATIONAL RECORD COLLECTOR'S CLUB: In addition to the publication of the Mapleson Cylinders (Section I.), and repressings from Victor masters, this organization published a 78.26 rpm disc made from acetates recorded from a radio broadcast over WQXR, New York City, 2 Feb., 1939. This was Eames' only radio broadcast.

IRCC 3142: Emma Eames comments on her records. (2 sides, 10" 78 rpm recording)

NOTES

The amateur discographer should *not* use the Eames discography as a key to the common practices of the Victor Talking Machine Company with respect to matrix numbering, assignment of catalog numbers, &c. as there are more things atypical in the Eames listings than any other single artist! Her recordings were made at certain transition points in factory policy, and for some reason the technicians made a number of errors in the assigning of numbers, and even more serious, in speed variations. Although Victor records varied in speed over the years, I know of no other case where a major Red Seal artist had two sessions which produced recordings made at the very slow speed of 72.73 (Discography Nos. 12, 34, 45, 46). These are some of Eames' best recordings, when reproduced at the correct speed, but the originals are among the most rare... presumably the public did not buy them, and one can understand why if they were tried out in the record shops at around 78 rpm! It was standard Victor policy to assign one matrix number to a selection, and this was used again and again for remakes of that title (as long as the accompaniment did not change); under this policy the *Cavalleria* remakes (No. 10) should have been numbered takes 3 & 4 of C-3388 (No. 9). The same holds true for the 1907 re-make of the *Don Giovanni* duet (No. 16) which should have been C-3170-3 (see No. 15), and with the Sembrich duets (Nos. 40 & 41). Several of the Eames records were apparently recorded with unusually broad styli; reproduction is difficult and may require some experimentation. Because of frequent substitution and re-use of numbers, the collector must be careful in the identification of the copies he holds. The following notes may help in this regard.

Discog.
No.

4. More of the original cylinder is heard on the Lp transcription than on the original 78 rpm issues.

9. Handwritten take (2) shows at 9 o'clock position in inner rim. Note the words "Ah, io piango..."

10. Handwritten take (2) at 9 o'clock position is underlined. Note the words "Ah, piango..."

13. 9th Mar. '06 pressings have handwritten matrix number (C-3172) at 6 o'clock and handwritten take (2) at 9 o'clock.
22nd May, '07 pressings do not have matrix number but have handwritten take number (3) at 9 o'clock.
6th Apr. '09 pressings have the catalog number 88183 (later used for a Johanna Gadski recording) crossed out at 6 o'clock.

14. A catalog number was assigned (later used for Pol Plançon) but the record was never issued as it was remade the following month with orchestra.

15. Handwritten matrix number and take show in inner rim. In the seventh measure de Gogorza sings: "...partiam ben mio..."

16. No matrix number or take show; in the seventh measure de Gogorza sings: "...partiam mio ben..."

42. Handwritten takes (2 & 4) appear at 9 o'clock on the respective pressings.

46. The original issue stated "accompaniment by Victor Orchestra" on the label; this is in error, as the record is with piano.

47. The record is labeled "Two American Patriotic Songs".

53. This is the only 10" recording in the Eames list. A catalog number was assigned but the recording was never issued, and no copies are known to exist.

54. The record is labeled "Pianoforte accompaniment by Henri Gilles" in error, as it is with orchestra.

Opera Biographies

An Arno Press Collection

Albani, Emma. **Forty Years of Song.** With a Discography by
W. R. Moran. [1911]

Biancolli, Louis. **The Flagstad Manuscript.** 1952

Bispham, David. **A Quaker Singer's Recollections.** 1921

Callas, Evangelia and Lawrence Blochman. **My Daughter
Maria Callas.** 1960

Calvé, Emma. **My Life.** With a Discography by W. R. Moran. 1922

Corsi, Mario. **Tamagno, Il Più Grande Fenomeno Canoro
Dell'Ottocento.** With a Discography by W. R. Moran. 1937

Cushing, Mary Watkins. **The Rainbow Bridge.** With a Discography
by W. R. Moran. 1954

Eames, Emma. **Some Memories and Reflections.** With a
Discography by W. R. Moran. 1927

Gaisberg, F[rederick] W[illiam]. **The Music Goes Round.** 1942

Gigli, Beniamino. **The Memoirs of Beniamino Gigli.** 1957

Hauk, Minnie. **Memories of a Singer.** 1925

Henschel, Horst and Ehrhard Friedrich. **Elisabeth Rethberg:**
Ihr Leben und Künstlertum. 1928

Hernandez Girbal, F. **Julian Gayarre:** El Tenor de la Voz
de Angel. 1955

Heylbut, Rose and Aimé Gerber. **Backstage at the Metropolitan
Opera** (Originally published as **Backstage at the Opera**). 1937

Jeritza, Maria. **Sunlight and Song:** A Singer's Life. 1929

Klein, Herman. **The Reign of Patti.** With a Discography by
W. R. Moran. 1920

Lawton, Mary. **Schumann-Heink:** The Last of the Titans. With a
Discography by W. R. Moran. 1928

Lehmann, Lilli. **My Path Through Life.** 1914

Litvinne, Félia. **Ma Vie et Mon Art:** Souvenirs. 1933

Marchesi, Blanche. **Singer's Pilgrimage.** With a Discography by
W. R. Moran. 1923

Martens, Frederick H. **The Art of the Prima Donna and Concert Singer.** 1923

Maude, [Jenny Maria Catherine Goldschmidt]. **The Life of Jenny Lind.** 1926

Maurel, Victor. **Dix Ans de Carrière, 1887-1897.** 1897

Mingotti, Antonio. **Maria Cebotari,** Das Leben Einer Sangerin. [1950]

Moore, Edward C. **Forty Years of Opera in Chicago.** 1930

Moore, Grace. **You're Only Human Once.** 1944

Moses, Montrose J. **The Life of Heinrich Conried.** 1916

Palmegiani, Francesco. **Mattia Battistini:** Il Re Dei Baritoni. With a Discography by W. R. Moran. [1949]

Pearse, [Cecilia Maria de Candia] and Frank Hird. **The Romance of a Great Singer.** A Memoir of Mario. 1910

Pinza, Ezio and Robert Magidoff. **Ezio Pinza:** An Autobiography. 1946

Rogers, Francis. **Some Famous Singers of the 19th Century.** 1914

Rosenthal, Harold [D.] **Great Singers of Today.** 1966

Ruffo, Titta. **La Mia Parabola:** Memorie. With a Discography by W. R. Moran. 1937

Santley, Charles. **Reminiscences of My Life.** With a Discography by W. R. Moran. 1909

Slezak, Leo. **Song of Motley:** Being the Reminiscences of a Hungry Tenor. 1938

Stagno Bellincioni, Bianca. **Roberto Stagno e Gemma Bellincioni Intimi** *and* Bellincioni, Gemma, **Io e il Palcoscenico:** Trenta e un anno di vita artistica. With a Discography by W. R. Moran. 1943/1920. Two vols. in one.

Tetrazzini, [Luisa]. **My Life of Song.** 1921

Teyte, Maggie. **Star on the Door.** 1958

Tibbett, Lawrence. **The Glory Road.** With a Discography by W. R. Moran. 1933

Traubel, Helen and Richard G. Hubler. **St. Louis Woman.** 1959

Van Vechten, Carl. **Interpreters.** 1920

Wagner, Charles L. **Seeing Stars.** 1940